FALLEN FROM GRACE

Understanding the Theology of Grace,
the Dangers of Legalism & the Three Phases of Apostasy

To Gary
"Be strong in the grace that is in Christ Jesus"

By

Charles E. Smoot

Aloha and Blessings
Charles E. Smoot
Maui 2005

xulon
PRESS

Fallen From Grace

Understanding the Theology of Grace,
the Dangers of Legalism & the Three Phases of Apostasy

Published by

Xulon Press

Printed in the United States of America

ISBN 1-591609-89-5

Xulon Press
www.XulonPress.com

Xulon Press books are available in bookstores everywhere, and on the Web at www.XulonPress.com.

To the memory of

" Grand Ma and Grand Pop "

Reverends Robert and Julia Smoot

" Preachers of the Gospel "

Who prayed and patiently waited for me to
come into knowledge of the gospel of the grace of God.

Grace Theology

The systematic interpretation
of the doctrines of grace
and their redemptive application
in the life of the believer,
through
the finished work of
the substitution and atonement
of Jesus Christ at Calvary.

Charles E. Smoot

Contents

Part I

LAW AND GRACE

PART II

JUSTIFICATION & THE STANDING OF THE BELIEVER

PART IV

PRESERVATION &
THE SECURITY OF THE BELIEVER

PART V

REPROBATION & THE DISQUALIFICATION OF THE BELIEVER

PART VI

APPROACHING THE THRONE OF GRACE

Acknowledgements

This book would not be complete without giving thanks to God for those who have helped to make this book a reality. In my heart, I know how much each of you has meant to me at various stages of the evolution of this work. You know who you are. I want you to know I could never have completed this book without you.

For your prayers, encouragement, inspiration and support, I wish to express my love, appreciation and thanks to:

Ellen Sherrill
Lori Lawson
Shawna Koon
Cathryn True
Nehemiah & Carol Brown
Kelly & Nancy Stillwell
Gloria Bennett
Tiffany Presley

Thank you, *Dr. James and Pastor Colleen Marocco* and all my wonderful friends at the *King's Cathedral* for your love, friendship, and encouragement.

Special thanks to *Ms. Beverly Kenner* who donated the computer and materials from which this manuscript was prepared and who labored generously in many ways to make this book a reality.

May God's grace be with you.

Preface

This book is only the first of a series that deal with the subject of *God's grace*. This work, ***Fallen from Grace,*** began as a simple Bible study to be shared during a weekly Bible class. It progressed to a series of lessons on *grace* that became rather lengthy and involved. All the while, *the Holy Spirit* was trying to get me to realize that my *"simple Bible study"* was actually a book He was prompting me to write.

Let me acknowledge at the outset that I do not consider myself an authority on *the doctrines of grace*. Whatever knowledge I am able to confer to the reader did not come to me from studying other works about the doctrines of *grace.* It is part of the revelation God began to give to me as a young pastor *15* years ago. He is still revealing his *grace* to me on a daily basis.

When God dealt with me to write this book, He also impressed me not to read other books on the subject of *grace* (I ran out and bought a few). He told me that He would speak directly to my *spirit* the message He wanted me to deliver. I was only able to draw from my former training, the Bible and the understanding of what God imparted directly to my spirit. I apologize, therefore, for the lack of a bibliography or references to the material of other writers who have formerly dealt with the subject of *grace*. For those of you who esteem scholarship, I hope to produce a more scholarly work on the subject in the future.

I wrote this book because I believe the Holy Spirit told me to do so. I am sure there are other great works out there that have already dealt in a measure with this subject. Here is my contribution to the *Body of Christ*. I hope this work will compel and challenge many to examine their theology and enable them to recognize *God's grace* as it flows into their own lives.

All of my life I have been a Pentecostal. I received the experience referred to as the *"baptism with the Holy Spirit"* in 1975 in Baltimore, Maryland when I was 17 years old. I have written this work for Pentecostals, Charismatics and others who have been told that *the road to heaven is paved with good works.* Instead, I have found that *the road to heaven is sprinkled with blood.* I realize that I am only one voice crying in the wilderness. May this book help to make His paths straight, and may it truly be to *the praise of the glory of his grace* (Eph. 1:6).

Introduction

How would you define *legalism*? What is *grace theology*? As the title suggests, this book is written to aid all believers in their understanding of God's marvelous *grace*. As we journey through its pages, a clear message will begin to unfold. We will delve into the lives of *grace believers* and *legalists* alike who lived under various *dispensations and covenants* found in both *Old and New Testaments.*

As I walk among the ranks of Christians of all denominations, I am aware that very few Christians truly embrace the fullness of *God's grace,* much less have a basic understanding of what it means to be *saved by grace.* I marvel even more when I find this is the case with many preachers. The study of *the theology of grace* is very important if we as believers are to live free of the power of sin, as well as the bondage of *condemnation* and *guilt* encouraged through *legalism.* In this work, I have attempted to answer some of the questions and controversy that surround *the doctrine of grace, legalism, and apostasy*. Such as:

- *What is legalism?*
- *What are the dangers of legalism?*
- *Are believers saved by faith or by works?*
- *Was Abraham justified by faith or by works?*
- *What does it really mean to be saved by grace?*
- *Just how secure is the believer's salvation?*
- *What does it really mean to fall from grace?*
- *What is a reprobate?*
- *Can a believer ever be eternally lost?*

As we journey throughout scripture, we will visit the *Garden of*

Eden, *the altars of Cain and Abel*, the *Tower of Babel*, *Mt. Moriah*, and explore other scenes where *grace* and *law* are revealed in *type and shadow*. We will wade with *John the Baptist* at the banks of the Jordan, and stand watch with Christ at the *Mount of Transfiguration.* We will compare the ministries and theology of *John the Baptist*, the *Pharisees*, *James and John,* the *sons of thunder,* and others, with the ministry of Christ.

Moreover, we will unlock the mystery of the seeming *contradiction of faith and works* as presented in the writings of the Apostle Paul and James, the brother of our Lord. To this end we might more fully understand what it means to truly know *Jesus Christ* in the fullness of *grace and truth.*

Legalism

Any belief system
where man derives merit
through the keeping of the law
or
other man-made doctrines,
disciplines, or rules
in order that he might obtain
righteousness with God
and thereby secure for himself
favor, blessings, and
in the end, salvation and eternal life.

PART I

LAW & GRACE

Tell me, ye that desire to be under the law, do ye not hear the law? For it is written, that Abraham had two sons, the one by a bondmaid, the other by a freewoman. But he who was of the bondwoman was born ***after the flesh****; but he of the freewoman was* ***by promise.***

Which things are an allegory: for these are the ***two covenants****; the one from the mount Sinai, which gendereth to bondage, which is Agar. For this Agar is* ***mount Sinai*** *in Arabia, and answereth to Jerusalem which now is, and is in bondage with her children. But* ***Jerusalem which is above*** *is free, which is the mother of us all. For it is written, Rejoice, thou barren that bearest not; break forth and cry, thou that travailest not: for the desolate hath many more children than she which hath an husband.*

Now we, brethren, as Isaac was, are ***the children of promise.*** *But as then he that was born after the flesh persecuted him that was born after the Spirit, even so it is now. Nevertheless what saith the scripture? Cast out the bondwoman and her son: for the son of the bondwoman shall not be heir with the son of the freewoman. So then, brethren, we are not children of the bondwoman, but of the free.*

Stand fast therefore in the liberty wherewith Christ hath made us free, and ***be not*** *entangled again with the yoke of bondage. Behold, I Paul say unto you, that if ye be circumcised, Christ shall profit you nothing. For I testify again to every man that is circumcised, that he is a debtor to do the whole law. Christ is become of* ***no effect*** *unto you,* ***whosoever of you are justified by the law; ye are fallen from grace.*** *For we through the Spirit wait for the hope of righteousness by faith.*

Galatians 4:21-5:5

1

Legalism

Since the dawn of history and in each age or dispensation thereafter, *man has always attempted to justify himself, to make himself holy, clean, acceptable and right with God.* In addition, man has always attempted to improve on God's plan of redemption. *Such attempts have always led man to some form of legalism.*

Since the beginning of the church and for nearly 2,000 years, there has also existed *a great debate* within—a theological *tug of war* between proponents of *law vs. grace and works vs. faith.* This book is about that struggle, a struggle that will continue until Jesus returns.

Legalism: A Religious Phenomenon

Legalism is *a religious phenomenon* within the Body of Christ. At the *core* of legalism is *the concept of righteousness through works.* For the purposes of this book, I would like to offer the following definition of works.

Works: ***righteous acts, deeds, effort, or service*** based on *human merit.*

Righteousness through works is *self-righteousness.* Self-righteousness and legalism are both *a curse and a stumbling block to the Body of Christ* (Rom. 9:31-33).

Legalism is responsible for more darkness and false teaching within the Body of Christ than anything else.

Legalism: The Yoke of Bondage

Merriam-Webster Dictionary defines *legalism* as ***strict, literal, or excessive conformity to the law or to a religious or moral code.*** For purposes of this work, I offer a definition of legalism:

Legalism is any belief system where man derives merit through the keeping of the law or other man-made doctrines, disciplines, or rules in order that he might obtain righteousness with God and thereby secure for himself favor, blessings, and in the end, salvation and eternal life.

Putting it simply—*Legalism is righteousness through works,* from which the apostle Paul admonishes "be not entangled again with the yoke of bondage" (Gal. 5:1). Some have mistakenly referred to "the yoke of bondage" in Galatians 5:1 as the bondage of sin. However, Paul, the apostle of grace tells us that:

The yoke of bondage is a direct biblical reference to being justified by keeping the Law of Moses and what is known today as legalism.

However, in spite of Paul's admonition, many are still "entangled" in legalism and *cannot free themselves* from that which they *"desire"* to be under (Gal 4:21). It is the same yoke, which the apostle Peter said, "neither we nor our father's were able to bear" (Acts 15:10).

What is A Legalist?

Now that we have a basic definition of legalism, I would like to offer a basic definition of a legalist. Merriam-Webster's Dictionary defines a legalist as *one that views things from a legal standpoint; especially: one that places primary emphasis on legal principles or on the formal structure of governmental institutions.* I would like to offer another definition of a legalist.

A legalist is one who deals with man from the basis of the law and not from the basis of grace.

A legalist's theology, ministry, and methods are often characterized by ***self-righteousness, judgment, and condemnation;*** *with little or no compassion, mercy, or redemption.*

A legalist *emphasizes the demand of the law* but *fails to see* the underlying principle or ideal for which it stands. We shall explain what we mean by this later.

2

The Two Covenants

For it is written, that Abraham had two sons, one by a bondmaid, the other by a free woman. But he who was of the bondwoman was born after the flesh, but he of the free woman was by promise. Which things are an allegory: for these are the two covenants;

(Gal. 4:22-24)

Which were born, not of blood, nor of the will of the flesh, nor of the will of man, but of God.

(Jn. 1:13)

That which is born of the flesh is flesh; and that which is born of the Spirit is spirit.

(Jn. 3:6)

Salvation—A Miracle of Grace

An allegory is an extended metaphor. It is *an illustration* used in scripture to *explain or give meaning* to a *biblical type, shadow,* or other spiritual truth. The Old Testament is full of types and shadows. The New Testament abounds with allegories. This allegory of *Isaac and Ishmael* illustrates the New Testament truth that:

Salvation is possible only because of the promise of God and not by the righteous efforts of man.

It further illustrates *the struggle* between the proponents of law and grace, "but as then he that was born after the flesh persecuted him that was born after the Spirit, even so it is now" (Gal. 4:29). In other words:

Those who, by the grace of God, put their trust solely in the blood of Jesus as the basis for salvation are persecuted by those who would look to themselves and to their own works in order to obtain and maintain righteousness with God.

I can find no better example of this than Paul's use of Isaac and Ishmael. Isaac was a child by *promise, born after* (or of) *the Spirit.* He was conceived by *grace through faith.* He was *a gift* to Abraham through Sarah (Gen. 15:1-6; Rom. 4:17-22). (Though Abraham was about 100 years old and Sarah was 90 and beyond the age of child-birth).

As *Isaac's birth was made possible because of a miracle of God's grace*, so is salvation made possible because of a miracle of God's grace.

Legalism—The Righteous Efforts of Man

Ishmael, on the other hand, was a child of *the will of man, born after the flesh.* He was conceived by works (or by the works of the flesh). He was conceived in *unbelie*f (Gen. 16:1,3,16). It was *unbelief* that necessitated his birth to begin with. Such unbelief could not embrace the promise of God. For Sarah did not believe the word God had spoken to her.

Therefore, Ishmael was not a gift (from above) promised by God, but *a reward* to Abraham through Hagar, an Egyptian slave. He was conceived of *the flesh* (or the will of man). *Ishmael was born of water* or of *the flesh and not of the Spirit or of promise* (Jn. 3:5-7; Gal. 4:28-29).

When Christ told Nicodemus, "**That which is born of the flesh is flesh**," he was referring to:

<u>*The origins of two births*</u>

- *One natural— One spiritual*
- *One of man—One of God*
- *One of this world—One not of this world*
- *One from earth—One from heaven*

For many years, I inferred from His conversation with Nicodemus that Christ was referring to *water baptism* because He mentions being *born of water. However, neither the text nor context mentions baptism at all.*

Many legalists have concluded that John 3:5 is an indirect reference to being baptized with water. However, the context of this verse *cannot* support this speculation at all.

Christ is not teaching water baptism here. *Christ is contrasting a natural birth of* ***the flesh*** *with that of* ***the Spirit*** *and teaching the necessity of a new birth (being born again) from above.* The Greek word used here for *again* is *anothen* and means *from above*. It is used of things which come from heaven or from God in heaven. We will have more to say on the subject of baptism later.

Law and Grace Incompatible

More than any other illustration, these two sons, *the allegory of their births, their enmity, their incompatibility to co-exist together, and their inability to both be heirs together of the same promise* made to Abraham *represent the two covenants of* ***law and grace***. They also *represent the enmity and incompatibility between those who are legalists and those who are grace believers.*

One would think that after nearly *2,000* years of growth, the church would have cast out this "bondwoman and her son" as Abraham did (Gal. 4:30). Instead, *the bondwoman and her sons remain with us alive and well to this day.*

Yet, we are encouraged to "grow in grace, and in the knowledge of our Lord and savior Jesus Christ" (2 Pet. 3:18).

Casting out the Son of the Bondwoman

..Cast out the bondwoman and her son: for the son of the bondwoman shall not be heir with the son of the freewoman.
(Gal. 4:30)

For a time, Ishmael and Isaac *existed in the same household, ate the same food, and shared the same blessings.* They had the same father but not the same mother. *Their births were different.* One was from *above*, and one was from the earth. However, as they grew up together *there eventually came a time when they had to separate.* The principle of the *type* is clear. *Legalism has to be cast out* (See also Gal. 4:24-26). Why must legalism be cast out? Because *law cannot co-exist with grace.*

Legalism Must Be Cast Out

Casting out the son of the bondwoman was not an easy thing to do. Ishmael was, after all, Abraham's son and half brother to Isaac. He was blood. As such, Abraham's heart was bound to the child by love. Yet, Abraham had to do something to correct the mistake he made in the flesh. A drastic measure was taken. Ishmael was cast out. *Abraham did this understanding the dangers ahead and to avert the trouble and confusion that would later ensue over the birthright and who would become his heir.* This was not only in the natural sense but also in the spiritual as well (Gen. 15:5).

At the request of his wife, Abraham made a hard choice. He made a good choice, for God told him to "hearken unto her voice" (Gen. 21:12). He regretfully and tearfully told Hagar and Ishmael they could no longer dwell among them.

Yet, in the spiritual realm, Satan is achieving the exact opposite in the Body of Christ today. *Legalism remains among us.* In fact:

Legalism is so entrenched in modern day theology that among certain ranks the sons of the bondwoman (legalists) ***outnumber and have more influence than the sons of the free*** (grace believers).

Make no mistake: It is the brethren who believe in grace who are being *troubled* and *persecuted by* those who hold on to *the yoke* of legalism (Acts 15:5, 24; Gal 4:29). This is exactly what Paul prophesied would happen! Something yet has to be done to bring the church back in line with the apostolic teaching of *grace* as taught by the apostle Paul. Something is being done! God has raised up a company of prophets to declare *the gospel of the grace of God* (Acts 20:24).

The dung of legalism must not be allowed to pollute the pure waters of *grace and truth* any longer. You can rest assured *that the legalist will put up a struggle to remain a viable member of the household.* He is, after all, family. Like Abraham and Sarah, you and I have a difficult choice to make. For the sake of the gospel, it must be made. The question remains—do we have the courage to make it? *Will the son of the bondwoman be heir with the son of the free?* In light of Paul's allegory of Isaac and Ishmael, one must honestly and sincerely ask:

- *Am I a child of the bondwoman or of the free?*
- *Am I a child of promise or of the work of the flesh?*
- *Am I a child of law or of grace?*
- *Am I a child of works or of faith?*
- *Am I saved by grace through works, or by grace through faith?*
- *Did I receive the promise of the Spirit through the hearing of the law or the hearing of faith?*
  (Gal. 3:14).

In other words—Is my salvation *a gift* or *a reward*? The inevitable answer must be: *If salvation is indeed a gift, then it is without merit.* This means that *one can do nothing to earn or deserve it.* If salvation is based on works, then it is based on the performance or righteousness of the one so saved. Thus, salvation becomes no gift at all but entirely a reward.

The Ever-Present Danger of Legalism

What is the ever-present danger of legalism?

Legalism removes grace from the gospel and replaces it with works. It turns the needy soul toward trusting in himself rather than in the blood of Jesus Christ.

Why Sarah Laughed!

When God told Sarah that she would receive a son by *promise* in her old age, Sarah laughed (Gen. 18:11-15)! The thought of having a child in her old age seemed as ridiculous as it seemed impossible.

Yet, *God demonstrated* **the power of his grace**. *He gave her* ***a gift without merit***. *He fulfilled His promise to Abraham in spite of her unbelief and her inability to conceive after the manner of women.* He gave her a son.

Isaac was a gift. He was a miracle of God's grace.

I ask you today—Has God found you laughing? *Is it so ridiculous that you can be saved by grace through faith, without works, self-righteousness, or the deeds of the law?* If so, then I invite you to read on.

Now we, brethren, as Isaac was, are children of promise...So then, brethren, we are not children of the bondwoman but of the free.

(Gal. 4:28,31)

3

<u>*The Law*</u>

Wherefore the law was our schoolmaster to bring us unto Christ, that we might be justified by faith. But after that faith is come, we are no longer under a schoolmaster.

(Gal. 3:24-25)

For the law having a shadow of good things to come, and not the very image of the things, can never with those sacrifices which they offered year by year continually make the comers thereunto perfect.

(Heb. 10:1)

For the law made nothing perfect, but the bringing in of a better hope did; by the which we draw nigh unto God.

(Heb. 7:19)

No Longer Under A Schoolmaster

Although the Old Testament *canon* of scripture *(Genesis - Malachi)* is referred to as *the law and the prophets*, the law specifically was the *moral, civil, and ceremonial code that was given to Moses as revealed in the first five books of the Bible known as the Pentateuch (Genesis - Deuteronomy).* Paul said this law was the ***handwriting of ordinances contained in commandments that was against us and contrary to us*** (Eph. 2:15; Col. 2:14).

It was *a covenant* given and enjoined to *the nation of Israel* approximately *1,500 years before Christ* and was still in force at the time Christ came. The law had a definite place in the unfolding plan of man's redemption. *Through the types and shadows of the law we are made to understand more fully the redemptive work of Jesus Christ* (Jn. 5:39). However:

The law as a covenant, with its strict demand for righteousness through obedience, was never intended to be the redemptive agent of man.

Furthermore, *it was never enjoined to the New Testament church* (Rom. 6:14). Although the law was *good, holy, and just,* and although *it proclaimed the righteousness of God and set a righteous standard for man, it did have a fault, in that it failed to provide man the righteousness it demanded* (Gal. 3:21). Why did the law fail? It failed because of man's sinful nature and propensity toward sin. In fact, the New Testament writers reveal the following truths about the law:

"Wherefore then serveth the law? It was **added** *because of transgressions* **till** *the seed should come..."*
(Gal. 3:19, emphasis added)

Regarding the law, we must first understand that *the law is a schoolmaster, a tutor, or teacher* (Gal. 3:24). We therefore *utilize the law to teach and to learn about Christ.* So, what does the law teach and what do we learn?

- ***The Moral Law:*** *revealed in the Ten Commandments teaches us concerning* **the righteousness of God.**

- ***The Civil Law:*** *revealed in the judgments teaches us concerning* **the sinfulness of man.**

- ***The Ceremonial Law:*** *reveals the need of* ***atonement for sin and reconciliation*** *between God and man.*

These provide us *types and shadows* of the atoning work of

Jesus Christ as revealed in the New Covenant.

What's Wrong with the Law?

For if that first covenant had been faultless, then should no place have been sought for the second. For finding ***fault*** *with them, he saith,* ***Behold, the days come, saith the Lord, when I will make a new covenant with the house of Israel and the house of Judah:*** (Heb. 8:7,8, emphasis added)

<u>*The Old Testament Law Has Faults*</u>

- *The law was* ***weak*** (Heb. 7:18)
- *The law was* ***unprofitable*** (Heb. 7:18)
- *The law* ***made nothing perfect*** (Heb. 7:19)
- *The law* ***was despised*** (Heb. 10:28*)*
- *The law* ***was for the time then present*** (Heb. 9:9-10)
- *The law* ***worketh wrath*** (Rom. 4:15)
- *The law* ***was without mercy*** (Heb. 10:28)
- *The law was the ministry* ***of condemnation*** (2 Cor. 3:9*)*
- *The law was the ministry* ***of death*** (2 Cor. 3:9*)*

The law with all of its glory had only *a shadow of good things to come* (Heb. 10:1). Those good things to come included the salvation and benefits of The New Covenant.

- ***<u>A shadow</u> in scripture is an Old Testament figure, outline, or pattern of an object*** (Heb. 8:5, 9:23-24). However, the law was *a shadow* and therefore ***not*** the real substance or object that cast the shadow.

- ***<u>A type</u> in scripture is an Old Testament representation of a promise or truth that is fulfilled in the New Testament.*** The Old Testament is the promise. The New Testament ***is*** the *fulfillment* of that promise. The apostle Paul tells us plainly that:

The fulfillment or object of the messianic types and shadows

which the law represented is Christ himself and the finished work he would accomplish at the cross (Col. 2:17).

More importantly, Paul also declares that:

As grace believers we are not under the Old Covenant of the law but under the New Covenant of grace (Rom. 6:14)!

Why is this so? Because ***after*** *that faith is come we are* ***no longer*** *under a schoolmaster* (Gal. 3:21-25). The law is fulfilled in Christ (Matt. 5:17).

I Am Not Come to Destroy, But to Fulfill

...These are the words which I spake unto you, while I was yet with you, that all things must be fulfilled, which were written in the law of Moses, and in the prophets, and in the psalms, concerning me...

And beginning at Moses and all the prophets, he expounded unto them in all the scriptures the things concerning himself.

(Lk. 24:44,27)

Think not that I am come to destroy the law, or the prophets: I am not come to destroy, but to fulfil.

(Matt. 5:17)

Mathew 5:17 is often misquoted by the legalist to justify legalism in its various forms, inferring that believers are under ***both*** covenants of *Law and Grace,* and that New Testament believers must (through the power of the Holy Spirit) keep the laws of the Old Testament. However, they miss the point. That is:

Christ came to fulfill the law in two ways.

1) Christ through his sinless life came ***to fulfill or satisfy the righteous demands of the law*** in man's behalf. *Christ came to fulfill or provide for man what the law demanded and promised but could not provide.*

2) Christ came to fulfill or be ***the embodiment of the types and shadows of the law***, as well as ***the messianic prophecies*** concerning him. He came to establish the law, ***declaring himself the fulfillment*** of each *prophetic type, shadow* and *promise* of the coming Messiah (Jn. 4:25-26).

Christ came to fulfill and to provide ***righteousness for us***. Christ became:

- ***The Just****: Jesus is the* ***only one*** *who lived and met the* ***standard*** *of righteousness that the law required.*

  Moreover, he became:

- ***The Justifier****: Jesus is the* ***only one*** *through whom* ***righteousness can be imputed*** *to those who put their trust in him* (Acts 3:14; Rom. 3:26).

The Law—A Shadow Of Things to Come

For the law having a shadow of good things to come, and not the very image of the things, can never with those sacrifices which they offered year by year continually make the comers thereunto perfect.

(Heb. 10:1)

Which are a shadow of things to come; but the body is of Christ.

(Col. 2:17)

It has been said that *the Old Testament is the New Testament concealed, and the New Testament is the Old Testament revealed.* Many preachers however have not properly understood the relationship between the *types and shadows* of the *Old Testament Law* and their *fulfillment* in the *New Testament of Grace* (Col. 2:17). When interpreting and applying the Old Testament scriptures today, they have ignored a very important principle of interpretation. That is:

As New Testament believers, we must interpret the types and shadows of the Old Testament Law from the standpoint of grace and we must not interpret grace from the standpoint of the law.

To understand ***grace theology*** we must progress in knowledge and revelation from the *revealed* truth in order to understand the *concealed truth.*

Just because we are first introduced to the shadow (the law) *does not mean that we use the shadow to interpret the object which it represents* (grace). Why?

A shadow *cannot* interpret or give meaning to the object that cast the shadow. However, *the object that casts the shadow interprets or gives meaning to the shadow.* In this case, a *shadow* (the law) *is a vague and ambiguous representation of something else* (grace).

No shadow can provide enough detail to reveal all there is to know about the object it represents. All we can expect are hints and clues. For example, the shadow of a person might not be clear enough to tell if it were a man or a woman, much less whom it is. The shadow of a plane or bird flying would not reveal its type. Even the shadow of a hand and two fingers cast upon the ground may appear to be a rabbit, a dog, or some other creature. *Until the object that cast the shadow is fully known or revealed, questions remain.* What color, how tall, deep or wide an object is will remain a mystery *until the object itself is in plain view.*

The shadow is only a *temporary representation and exists because there is a true object that cast the shadow.* Likewise:

We can only interpret the law as we fully know Christ as revealed in the New Covenant of grace.

Similarly, as the Old Testament believers had only the law, we are unable to interpret what we see because it is only *a shadow of good things to come*. Nevertheless, if we follow the shadow it will lead us to its source. In other words the law is intended to **"bring us unto Christ that we might be justified by faith"** (Gal. 3:24).

The unknown or concealed truth in this instance consists of the types and shadows of the law itself. That is why we refer to them *as types and shadows*, because they *represented* something else—something *yet* to come. The revealed or known truth in this instance is that:

Jesus Christ, His finished work of atonement and the New Covenant of grace, are the true objects that cast the shadows into the Old Testament.

If we can understand this, our understanding of *grace theology* is much clearer. ***The law with its types and shadows does not interpret grace,*** *but rather,* ***grace interprets the law.*** Grace, therefore, is the true object *known only by revelation*, and *the law is merely the shadow of grace not yet revealed or made known.* You see, the Bible tells us very plainly that the law is our "schoolmaster [tutor] to bring us to Christ" (Gal. 3:24). However:

The legalist preaches Christ to bring believers under the yoke of the law (Acts 15:10). *Legalism makes Christ the shadow and the law the fulfillment or object of truth.*

Legalism removes the believer from Calvary and the grace of God and takes him back to Sinai to the yoke of bondage.

The legalist might begin his message at Calvary, but eventually will end up at Sinai. However:

The grace believer preaches the law to bring men to Christ. Grace theology makes the law the shadow and Christ the object of truth.

Grace theology removes men from Sinai and the bondage of the law, takes them to Calvary, and plants them in *the grace of God.* Remember, if we follow the shadow (the law), it will lead us to its source (Christ) (Gal. 3:24).

The grace preacher may begin his message at Sinai or from the Old Testament, but he will always end up at Calvary. For example:

When preaching Christ from the Old Testament — *Philip, Paul, and Aquila used the law to bring others to Christ* (Gal. 3:24-25; Acts 8:32-35, 17:2-3, 18:28). ***They did not preach Christ for the law's sake; they preached the law for Christ's sake.*** They *used* the law *to show that Jesus was the Christ because he was the only person in history who could truly fulfill all the types, shadows and prophecies given in the Old Testament concerning the Messiah.* When preaching to the Ethiopian Eunuch, *Philip understood that the lamb brought to the slaughter and the sheep shorn in Isaiah 53 was none other than Jesus* (Isa. 53:7; Acts 8:32-35)! Likewise, as grace believers we must use the law to preach Christ and not use Christ to preach the law!

We Have Found Him!

Philip findeth Nathanael, and saith unto him, We have found him, of whom Moses in the law, and the prophets, did write, Jesus of Nazareth, the son of Joseph.

(Jn. 1:45)

Paul says that when we find the source, we have found the true object itself and have no further need for a *schoolmaster* (the law). Therefore, to those who are in Christ, *the law is no longer in force today.* Paul says, the law is *abolished, decayeth, waxeth old and is ready to vanish away* (2 Cor. 3:13; Heb. 8:13).

The law has served its purpose. It has brought us to Christ. In spite of what the legalist may say, we are ***no longer*** *under the law, but under grace* (Rom. 6:14; Gal. 3:24-25). In *grace* we find Christ full of *grace and truth* (Jn. 1:14). No wonder Philip could say, "We have found him, of whom Moses in the law, and the prophets, did write, Jesus of Nazareth, the son of Joseph." Philip identified Jesus as the Christ, because the Old Testament scriptures testified of him (Jn. 5:39). *Philip not only used the law to bring his brother Nathaniel to Christ, he also used the law to bring the Ethiopian Eunuch to Christ* (Acts 8:32-35).

When we preach from the Old Testament, we must preach the mysteries of Christ and the grace and truth that are in Him, and

not the legalism of the law.

Instead, many preachers today do not preach Christ except to bring people into the bondage of legalism. This is wrong. *The Judaizers and Pharisees of Paul's day made this same mistake in regards to circumcision and the keeping of the Sabbath day* (Acts 15:1; Mk. 2:23-24). They were zealous for the law of God, yet they lacked spiritual understanding. *They focused their ministry on the shadow rather than the object that cast the shadow.*

The legalist is making the same error today in regard to the new birth, baptism, the Sabbath, rules regarding apparel, the wearing of makeup and jewelry, length of hair, food and drink, television, movies, and a host of other things they believe essential for salvation and righteous standing with God.

The grace believer understands that God intended that the law should serve Christ and not that Christ should serve the law. For it is written "..the elder [the law] shall serve the younger [grace]" (Rom. 9:12). Jesus understood this principle when he corrected the Pharisees by saying, "the Sabbath was made for man, and not man for the Sabbath" (Mk. 2:27).

4

Grace

John bare witness of him, and cried, saying, This was he of whom I spake, He that cometh after me is preferred before me: for he was before me.

And of his fullness have all we received, and grace for grace.
(Jn. 1:15-16)

The Forerunner

After *400* silent years, a man stepped from the wilderness gate and began to preach in *the spirit and power of Elijah* the prophet (Lk. 1:17). His life was full of mystique and mystery, for he had come from obscurity. He wasn't a company man, or a card-carrying Pentecostal preacher. He didn't belong to the *"good old boys"* club. For God had sent this man.

The wilderness had been his seminary. There, he was kept "till the day of his shewing to Israel" (Lk. 1:80). A solitary man, he lived a solitary existence. He owned no real estate, had neither wife nor family; he was clothed in camel's hair and ate wild locusts and honey. His name was *John.*

John the Baptist was the last of the Old Testament prophets and the first of the New. I have often wondered if John were to walk among us today, would we recognize his ministry and honor him as a prophet of God?

A Message of Truth

When we compare the ministries of John and Jesus, we see very little similarity. Why? John the Baptist came with a message. His ministry was only a message of truth. He did not have a ministry of grace. *The message of John was both prophetic and legalistic (based on the law) in nature.* Although he proclaimed, "..Prepare ye the way of the Lord, make His paths straight" (Matt. 3:3), he also said to Herod, "..It is not lawful for thee to have thy brother's wife" (Mk. 6:18). Why is this significant?

John, like his predecessors, could not preach grace because that was reserved for those who would come with a ministry of *grace and truth.* This ministry was ushered in with Christ and the Apostles. Yet, *the ministry of the prophet is very compelling.* However, *the dispensation or age of the law* (the righteousness of God) *and the prophets* (the need for repentance) *were (only) until John.* Since that time, "the kingdom of God is preached, and every man presseth into it" (Lk. 16:16).

This is not to say that righteousness and repentance are not needed today. Neither are we saying that they should not be preached.

If there was ever a time to preach righteousness and repentance, it is today. We are simply saying that we now have **"a better covenant... established on better promises"** (Heb. 8:6). *This better covenant has made it possible for all men to enter into the kingdom (being saved) without the works of the law.*

There Cometh One Mightier Than I

Like his predecessors, John prophesied *of the grace that should come to us* (1 Pet. 1:10). He said," ..There cometh one mightier than I after me, the latchet of whose shoes I am not worthy to stoop down and unloose" (Mk. 1:7). On another occasion he said, "there standeth one among you, whom ye know not; He it is, who coming after me is preferred before me" (Jn. 1:26-27).

John declared that, "he [Jesus] must increase, but I must

decrease" (Jn. 3:30). What he was really saying is that *the age of the law* is about to end. John, the last Old Testament prophet, came to draw the curtain closed for the final act and proclaim Jesus "the lamb of God that taketh away the sin of the world" (Jn. 1:29). Therefore, after the baptism of Jesus and John's validation of Christ's ministry, John's ministry enters the twilight. Soon, he will be gone and Jesus will usher in a new age, the church age, the age of grace and truth.

Therefore, John's ministry lasted for only *six months*, and Christ's ministry for three and a half *years*. It is said of John, "John did no miracle" (Jn. 10:41). This I believe was done on purpose to reveal *the redemptive aspect of grace*. It testifies to the fact that *Christ has a better ministry, far exceeding the ministry of the law.* He had not only a message, but he also had a ministry of mercy. For he *was full of grace and truth* (Jn. 1:14,17).

I began my ministry as a *Pentecostal* preacher at the age of *twenty*. Like many before me, I gladly received *the mantle of Elijah, the tablets of Moses,* and strove to preach Christ. Not realizing:

I had one foot firmly planted on Sinai and the other slipping from Calvary.

I was caught in *the mire of legalism*. Like John, for many years all I had was a message of truth. Oh yes, it was a compelling message. I proclaimed *the righteousness of God*, *the sinfulness of man*, and stressed *repentance, obedience, and a life of personal holiness*. With this I strove to preach Christ as best I could. However, it was not until many years later I received the revelation that would set me free. I received the revelation of *the ministry of grace and truth*. This revelation changed my life.

The Ministry of Grace and Truth

For the law was given by Moses, but grace and truth came by Jesus Christ.

(Jn. 1:17)

Thou therefore, my son, be strong in the grace that is in Christ Jesus.

(2 Tim. 2:1)

The law may be *lawful* and it certainly is *expedient*, but there is one thing about the law we must all come to realize sooner or later. We must realize that *the law is not redemptive.* So:

Why then do men appeal to that which cannot save, empower, restore, or preserve the believer?

As I struggled to find a balance within my own life and ministry, the Holy Spirit did a wonderful thing. He gave me a *revelation* and an understanding of *the theology of grace*. This revelation has changed much of my theology and continues to transform my life as well. It is my belief that:

God intended that grace and truth should work together to accomplish the redemption of man.

The psalmist spoke of a time *when mercy and truth are met together; righteousness and peace have kissed each other* (Psa. 85:10). That time arrived when Jesus Christ shed his precious blood and gave his Spirit to the believer.

Many preachers do not have the revelation or the understanding of the grace that is in Christ Jesus. They seek to bring the demands of the law into the dispensation of grace, and use the law as an example of how God deals with sin and disobedience. However, this is a serious mistake and will lead men into the bondage of legalism and other false doctrines.

As we shall see:

It is incorrect to misapply Old Testament scriptures and principles to New Testament theology. Yet, many preachers continue to deal with people from the basis of the law and not from the basis of grace.

One rule of thumb is to remember that:

Jesus dealt with people from the basis of grace, not from the basis of the law. Jesus dealt with people from a remedial, redemptive standpoint and not a legal standpoint.

Jesus granted *favor, blessing, healing, deliverance, forgiveness, and salvation all on the basis of his grace alone, n*ever once with a single demand of the law. His goal was to save, not to judge or punish. Jesus is the essence and fullness of grace and truth. He is *grace and truth personified.* Remember, Jesus is *the Word made flesh,* He is one with God the Father (Jn. 1:14; 10:30).

Throughout his ministry, Jesus demonstrated how mistaken men can be (though they mean well) when they appeal to *the law and the prophets* for direction and not to his example of New Testament *grace ministry.* Two examples are found in John chapter 8 and Luke chapter 9.

An Appeal to the Law & The Prophets

And the scribes and the Pharisees brought unto him a woman taken in adultery; and when they had set her in the midst,

They say unto him, Master, this woman was taken in adultery, in the very act.

Now Moses in the law commanded us, that such should be stoned: but what sayest thou?

(Jn. 8:3-5)

The *ministry of grace and truth* can be clearly seen in the account of *the woman taken in adultery* as found in John's gospel. We have all heard sermons preached many times from these verses. Almost every time, the emphasis is on *not being a judge of other men's sins, or admonishing believers not to continue in sin after being saved.* I agree with this teaching. However, there is a deeper meaning here. If you look closely, you will see:

The compassionate, redemptive nature of our Lord's ministry, in contrast *to the unmerciful, judgmental, and legalistic ministry of the Pharisees of Jesus' day.*

The Pharisees

The Pharisees were what I refer to as *classical legalists*. Jesus called them *hypocrites*. Therefore, not having *the Spirit of grace* or the *heart* of God, they could only appeal to *Moses* (or to the law) for dealing with this situation. However, it appears they had an ulterior motive for coming to Jesus. They wanted to trap him that they might have an accusation against him. Instead, they were the ones who were trapped! Little did they know, they were about to learn a lesson they would never forget.

The Romans (under which the Holy Land was governed) had banned the Jews from administering capital punishment. Since it was *unlawful* for the Jews to put anyone to death, it is unclear whether they would have stoned the woman, although it appears from the words of Jesus, "Let him who is without sin among you first cast a stone at her," that they were prepared to do so (Jn. 8:7). In any case, *the Pharisees wanted the Law of Moses to prevail in condemning the woman.* They only brought her to Jesus that they might accuse him of blasphemy, and bring him into condemnation for teaching contrary to Moses' law.

The Pharisees had taken up stones to stone Jesus on occasion and were probably prepared to stone both Jesus and the woman. It is interesting that the woman's partner in sin was absent and was not brought to be condemned by Jesus. Perhaps, he already lay beneath a pile of stones. The scriptures do not say. Suffice it to say, Jesus was aware of their hypocrisy and gave them a valuable lesson in *grace theology.*

An Appeal to Moses

Since the Pharisees were also doctors and teachers of the law, they chose to appeal to Moses (the Law of Moses) as the basis for passing judgment on the woman. This they were obliged to do. To the Pharisees, the Law of Moses was supreme. *Had they not come to Jesus, their theology would never have been challenged. They would have continued in administering the law in the lives of the people, and they would never have seen the ministry of grace and truth in action.* However, everything was about to change with one question and one answer.

Now Moses in the law commanded us, that such should be stoned: but what sayest thou ?
(Jn. 8:5)

Jesus had them right where he wanted them. Without violating the law or condemning Moses, *He dealt with the real issues, which the law was unable to do.* He dealt with *the heart or the spirit of the matter.* Christ compelled them to see that they were just as guilty of sin as the woman. He did this with one answer.

He that is without sin among you, let him first cast a stone at her
(Jn. 8:7)

Suddenly, those who had been motivated by *self-righteousness and legalism found themselves accused, convicted, and condemned by their own conscience.* The accusers were themselves found guilty. Jesus simply spoke, stooped down, and wrote on the ground. When he stood up, the woman's accusers had vanished!

Such is the hypocrisy and guilt of any one who would dare lay anything to the charge of God's elect. For it is indeed Christ who died for them. Yea rather, that is risen again because of their justification (Rom. 8:33-34). How powerful that word of grace must have been! You see:

Grace theology deals with the attitudes of the heart, attitudes that are not seen. "*...for the LORD seeth not as man seeth; for man looketh on the outward appearance, but the LORD looketh on the heart* (1 Sam.16:7). Jesus is interested in what's in a man's heart—his *motives.*

The law does not deal with the heart and motives of man, only the after effects. This is why Jesus gave us the *Sermon on the Mount and the Beatitudes.* The Jews already had the Law of Moses. They had it for *1500* years. He wanted to introduce them to grace theology. *Grace theology is heart theology; grace theology is kingdom theology; grace theology* suggests that:

Sin is an outward manifestation of an inward spiritual condi-

tion or attitude of the heart.

Grace theology reveals that the act of sin is not nearly as important as what prompted or motivated the act in the first place. For example, adultery *is preceded by lust or covetousness. Murder is preceded by anger, hatred, or malice, etc.* (Matt. 5:21-28). Where do these attitudes reside? In the heart.

Legalism, on the other hand, is not concerned with the heart. Neither is it concerned with administering mercy and compassion.

5

Grace Ministry

..Neither do I condemn thee: go, and sin no more.
(Jn. 8:11)

Let not mercy and truth forsake thee:
(Prov. 3:3)

With these words, Jesus gave us *a perfect model for New Testament ministry today.* This model illustrates *the effectiveness of grace and truth working together in a redemptive way.* The order in which grace and truth are administered is also important.

- When Jesus told the woman, *"Neither do I condemn thee,"* He was imparting *grace* in the form of mercy.

- When Jesus told the woman, *"Go and sin no more,"* He was imparting *truth* in the form of a message.

I refer to this type of ministry as *grace ministry*. In grace ministry, the word of grace (neither do I condemn thee) goes hand in hand with the word of truth (go and sin no more). Why is this? I believe that this further illustrates that:

In matters of redemption, grace is greater than the law.

The ministry of grace and truth together can accomplish that which truth alone cannot accomplish.

For example:

Truth can expose and convict of sin, but only grace can provide a remedy or cure for sin.

You see, redemption flows from the grace of God—not from truth. That which changes a man's heart and sets him apart to God (sanctification) *flows from the union of grace and truth.*

Only grace and truth working together can transform a person's life. *The redemptive element of grace makes forgiveness and salvation possible. Without the element of grace, redemption and sanctification through the truth would not be possible* (Jn. 17:17).

Again, the scripture is fulfilled, "Mercy and truth are met together; righteousness and peace have kissed each other" (Psa. 85:10). Herein is a valuable lesson for the church and the *five-fold ministry* today. That is:

Those with a ministry of grace and truth will never be subject to those who have only truth (a message).

Remember the words of *John the Baptist*. He said that He that would *come after* him with grace and truth is *mightier* and *preferred before* him. Understanding this, we can see that John had a message of truth, but he did not have a ministry of truth accompanied with mercy.

In summary, the Pharisees relied upon that which John relied upon — *the law*. When they left the woman, she was in the presence of one greater than Moses and the law. Perhaps they realized in some small way but did not fully understand that:

- *All have sinned and are guilty of the law.*
- *The law and legalism cannot deliver the guilty.*
- *Only God's grace stands between the demands of the law and the guilty.*
- *Grace is greater than the law and legalism.*
- *Mercy is greater than judgment.*
- *In Christ Jesus, we are free from the demands and penalty of the law.*

- *If the Son shall make you free, ye shall be free indeed.*

My dear minister friends, go ahead and preach your message. But if it does not have grace, your ministry will be compelling and convincing, but it will not be redemptive.

An Appeal to the Prophets

And when his disciples James and John saw this, they said, Lord, wilt thou that we command fire to come down from heaven, and consume them, even as Elias did?

(Lk. 9:54)

There is another important aspect of grace ministry I would like to introduce here. That is:

Having the right spirit and the right motivation for ministry

Previously, we examined an appeal to Jesus in the name of *"Moses."* Let us look briefly at an appeal to Jesus in the name of *"Elias."*

In scripture, *Moses and Elijah represent the law and the prophets.* It was Moses and Elijah who appeared *in glory* with Jesus on the *Mount of Transfiguration.* We shall look at the significance of this event a little later. Let's turn our attention to James and John and their startling request. Here, we have another important lesson in *grace theology.*

In our last example, the Pharisees were the legalists. In this lesson we shall look *at two apostles who early in their ministries were also legalists!* Does that surprise you? Is that possible? Of course it is. Remember:

A legalist is one who deals with man from the basis of the law and not from the basis of grace. His ministry is characterized by judgment and condemnation, and not by mercy or redemption.

The Sons of Thunder

James and John were such men. In fact, they were called *the sons of thunder* (Mk. 3:17). This gives some insight into their individual temperament. They were among the twelve Apostles and were formerly disciples of *John the Baptist*. In addition to the *70,* they were sent forth to preach the gospel of the kingdom (Lk. 10:1,9).

One day after they had preached in *Samaria,* they were rejected *en-masse* by the people. When they returned to Jesus and told him that Samaria had rejected their ministry, they inquired as to whether the Samaritans should be punished for their error. *They then appealed to Jesus in the name of Elijah the prophet, that they should "command fire to come down from heaven and consume them..." as Elijah had done!*

Spirit of the Law or Spirit of Grace?

But he turned and rebuked them, and said, Ye know not what manner of spirit ye are of.

For the Son of man is not come to destroy men's lives, but to save them...

(Lk. 9:55-56)

James and John were not prepared for what happened next. Rather than praise or approval, they were openly rebuked! In doing so, Jesus revealed to them that something was terribly wrong with their ministry.

Jesus rebuked them for their lack of compassion and mercy.

He rebuked them because they did not have or represent his true character and nature. The heart of the matter was:

- *They lacked the right spirit.*
- *They lacked the heart of God.*
- *They lacked the right motivation for ministry.*

Salvation is the heart of grace theology and the goal of grace ministry.

Jesus clearly stated his purpose in coming to this world and gave the right motivation for all ministry done in his name. He came *not to destroy men's lives, but to save them* (Lk. 9:55-56).

What Manner of Spirit?

What spirit did James and John have? Where did they get it? James and John had *the spirit of the law.* Legalism!

Allow me to share with you how God began to deal with me about the ministry of grace and truth. One evening, several years ago while in prayer, the Holy Spirit spoke to me the exact words that Jesus spoke to James and John, *"Ye know not what manner of spirit ye are of."* Again, He spoke to me and said, *"spirit of the law, or Spirit of grace."*

Immediately, the Holy Spirit began to deal with my heart and showed me *the difference between the condemnation of preaching with the spirit of the law and the redemption of preaching with the Spirit of grace.* I was so moved and changed by this experience that my ministry was transformed from that day forward.

The Spirit of the Law

Just what do we mean when we refer to *the spirit of the law*? The spirit of the law is *the spirit of judgment and condemnation. It is the spirit of legalism.*

The spirit of the law will often manifest as a spirit of self-righteousness. It is the demand for righteousness and of judgment without compassion and mercy. The spirit of the law is the heart of the legalist's theology and fuels the legalist's message.

Though the law has been abolished, *the spirit of the law* woefully is alive and doing well. When I refer to *the spirit of the law,*

I am not referring to the positive spirit of the Word that gives life and understanding to the true meaning and purpose of the law.

I am referring to the *negative, legalistic, exalted, self- righteous and judgmental spirit* which some manifest as they minister to the needs of man with only a ministry of truth.

The early ministry of James and John teaches us a few things

- *One can have the* ***right message but the wrong spirit.***
- ***Compassion*** *and* ***mercy*** *are the heart of God.*
- *Preaching and ministry must be done in a* ***redemptive*** *manner with* ***salvation*** *and not judgment in mind.*

One may be called, anointed and sent, but be impotent in administering *the gospel of the grace of God* (Acts 20:24). In doing so, one can appeal to Moses, Elijah, or whomever one wishes, but friend,

If you minister with the wrong spirit you can expect nothing less than the displeasure of Jesus with your ministry.

6

The Unveiling of Grace

But if the ministration of death, written and engraven in stones, was glorious, so that the children of Israel could not steadfastly behold the face of Moses for the glory of his countenance; which glory was to be done away: How shall not the ministry of the spirit be rather glorious?

For if the ministry of condemnation be glory, much more doth the ministry of righteousness exceed in glory. For even that which was made glorious had no glory in this respect, by reason of the glory that excelleth. For if that which was done away was glorious, much more that which remaineth is glorious.

(2 Cor. 3:7-11)

And not as Moses, which put a veil over his face, that the children of Israel could not steadfastly look to the end of that which is abolished:

But their minds were blinded: for unto this day remaineth the same veil untaken away in the reading of the old testament; which veil is done away in Christ.

But even unto this day, when Moses is read the veil is upon their heart.

Nevertheless when it shall turn to the Lord, the veil shall be taken away.

(2 Cor. 3:13-16)

But we all with open face beholding as in a glass the glory of the Lord, are changed into the same image from glory to glory ..

And not as Moses, which put a vail over his face, that the children of Israel could not steadfastly look to the end of that which is abolished:

But their minds were blinded: for unto this day remaineth the same veil untaken away in the reading of the old testament; which veil is done away in Christ.

(2 Cor. 3:13-14)

Mount Sinai or Mount Calvary?

There are at least *two ways one may approach the interpretation and application of scripture.* One may approach the scriptures from ***the perspective of Sinai*** or from ***the perspective of Calvary***. One may approach *from* ***the vantage point of the law*** or *from* ***the vantage point of grace.***

Each *vantage point* gives us an entirely different *perspective* from which we formulate our theology. One leads the believer to *the principle of justification by works.* The other leads the believer to *the principle of justification by faith.*

<u>The Vantage Point of Law and Grace</u>

- *Sinai* ⟶ *The Law* ⟶ *Justification By Works*
- *Calvary* ⟶ *Grace* ⟶ *Justification By Faith*

The vantage point from which you see or view truth is actually more important than the truth itself. For it holds *the keys* to interpretation.

Many false teachings have been perpetuated in the Body of Christ because men who meant well examined the scriptures from a legalistic works perspective, rather than from the redemptive perspective of grace. In short, they preached the gospel from Sinai and not from Calvary.

This is a very important distinction if we are to understand truth and apply it in a practical, redemptive way. The problem remains, however, that many ministers and Christians have been beholding *the New Testament doctrine of grace* through *the eyes of the spirit of the law* for so long, they are unable to clearly see and understand *the theology of grace* just as *the Jews and Judaizers* (legalists) of Paul's day. They are looking through a *veil.*

The Veil

As the Israelites could not behold the glory of Moses' countenance because of a veil,

The spirit of the law has become a veil to the legalist.

When Moses came down from Mount Sinai with *the law, written and engraven in stones, his face reflected the glory of God. That glory was upon both he and the law,* so that the children of Israel *could not steadfastly behold the face of Moses for the glory of his countenance* (2 Cor. 3:7). This glory not only *prevented* the people from seeing Moses' face, it also prevented Moses from being able to communicate the law to the people.

To remedy this, Moses covered his face with a veil. He could then instruct them in the law without their being afraid. Notice, however, *the veil was upon Moses and not upon the two tablets of stone.*

A veil is a shroud or covering. Paul explains that *this veil represents or is typical of* ***spiritual blindness*** *or* ***a lack of spiritual understanding****. This veil prevents not only Israel, but others as well from seeing the glory of God in the face of Jesus Christ* (2 Cor. 4:6). *But their minds were blinded.* Though their minds were blinded, notice where Paul says the veil is —the *veil is upon the heart, so that when the law is read, the mind is not illuminated and the heart cannot understand* (2 Cor. 3:14-15).

Today, ***this same veil is upon the heart of the legalist and prevents him from seeing and communicating the gospel of the grace of God*** (Acts 20:24). Paul explains, "for unto this day remaineth the same veil untaken away in the reading of the Old Testament" (2 Cor. 3:14).

That is, though they read the scriptures, their minds were

blinded because the veil is upon their heart, so that they cannot see the glory of Christ or understand *the grace of God*. There are many examples of those who could not see Christ because of this veil upon the heart (Lk. 24:25-27,44-45; Acts 7: 51, 8:34-35, 13:27).

The veil of the spirit of the law encourages legalism, self-righteousness, judgment and condemnation.

This veil has always been an obstacle to administering *compassion and mercy in dealing with others*. More importantly, *this veil (the spirit of the law) continues to keep many from seeing and understanding the New Covenant of the grace of God, and as a result,* ***legalism and false doctrines pervade the Body of Christ, alienating and separating believers one from another.***

The Principle of Interpretation of Scripture

The principle of interpretation of scripture is very important. As stated earlier,

Bible doctrines take on different meanings depending on which perspective or vantage point you view them.

When we examine the scriptures through the veil of *the spirit of the law* we are prone to misinterpret and misapply them. The result is false doctrine that leads men into *the yoke of bondage* called legalism (Gal. 5:1). That's what Paul was saying to us in Galatians when he warned us about *falling from grace.*

When warning us about falling from grace, Paul was not referring to ***"falling into sin"*** as some mistakenly teach. The context has nothing to do with sin.

Paul was warning believers against falling from the doctrinal position of salvation through grace alone and being entangled again with the yoke of legalism or the principle of righteousness through works (Gal. 5:4)!

The Vantage Point Of Sinai

Individual scriptures make up or comprise *doctrine* (Isa. 28:9-10). If doctrines are developed from scripture from the vantage point *of Sinai and the law*, those doctrines will reflect the *spirit* of the law.

The spirit of the law is to condemn.

When you add to this scenario a preacher who also has *the spirit of the law* and preaches from Sinai, *both his ministry and his message will be legalistic. He will preach scriptures that speak of grace, but he will not fully understand, communicate, or apply them in a practical, redemptive way.*

The Vantage Point Of Calvary

If doctrines are developed from scripture from the vantage point of Calvary and grace theology, those doctrines will reflect *the Spirit of grace* (Heb. 10:29).

The Spirit of grace is to pardon.

If the minister is himself transformed by grace and preaches from Calvary, *his ministry and his message will be redemptive. He will understand, communicate and apply grace theology in a practical, redemptive way.*

It is clear from Paul's writing that the only way to be rid of this veil of legalism is for *the heart of the preacher to turn to the Lord.* It is only then that the veil of *the spirit of the law* shall *be taken away* (2 Cor. 3:15-16).

I remember the night the Lord took the veil away from my heart. Since that night over fifteen years ago, every word I have spoken in the name of the Lord has been from Calvary. I could never go back to legalism.

Grace and The Sermon on the Mount

For I say unto you, That except your righteousness shall exceed the righteousness of the scribes and Pharisees, ye shall in no case enter into the kingdom of heaven.

(Matt. 5:20)

But seek ye first the kingdom of God, and his righteousness; and all these things shall be added unto you.

(Matt. 6:33)

Without the Spirit of grace, one will easily slip into the yoke of legalism and scarcely be able to cast it off.

Even the doctrines of the *election, justification, and the preservation of the believer* can be understood when examined with the *Spirit of grace* from the vantage point of Calvary. Why is this so? Simply because,

These processes are not based on the will and effort of man, but on the power and promises of God.

While on the other hand—*if examined from Sinai with the spirit of the law, these doctrines will be misunderstood, leading man to legalism and salvation through works.*

One of the best examples of the misinterpretation of scripture and the doctrinal problems that arise when viewing the scriptures from Sinai can be seen in reconciling *Matthew 5:20* and *Matthew 6:33*. Jesus, during the *Sermon on the Mount,* spoke these words. However, in this setting, Jesus contrasts his interpretation of *the Law* and *righteousness* with that of traditional thinking.

Interpreting these scriptures from a legalist's perspective gives rise to serious doctrinal error, taking the believer away from grace, Calvary, and the blood; and perpetuates legalism's doctrine of self-righteousness through works.

This error is further compounded from scripture to scripture, until the legalist has constructed *a chain of scriptural errors, pointing souls away from salvation by grace and righteousness through faith in the blood alone.* This is all possible because:

The legalist views and interprets scripture from Sinai and not from Calvary.

Greater and Better Works?

The legalist reasons from the above scriptures: Here—we have the disciple's righteousness contrasted against that of the scribes and Pharisees. The legalist immediately *compares their works* (of righteousness) and reasons:

"Except my works (of righteousness) are greater and better than the Pharisees, I will not be saved."

In other words:

The legalist feels compelled to ***"do something"*** *in order to raise or bring his life and conduct to a certain righteous standard.*

Then and only then can the legalist be assured he will be saved! On the other hand, interpreting *Matthew 5:20* and *Matthew 6:33* from the perspective of Calvary through *the principle of grace* reveals that:

The righteousness of man falls far short of the righteousness of God. Therefore, the believer must look outside of himself for righteousness in order to be saved.

- *The believer is* **pointed away** *from the works of his own righteousness, which is inadequate in the sight of God to save him.*

- *The believer is* **pointed to** *God that the believer might seek* ***"his righteousness"*** *which is greater than the self-righteousness of the scribes and Pharisees and which is more than adequate to save him.*

During the *Sermon on the Mount*, Christ taught the multitude that in order to enter *the kingdom of heaven*, man must seek the righteousness *imputed* from God, which is greater than that of *the scribes and Pharisees.*

As New Testament believers, through grace we understand that we are not to trust in our own works of righteousness as the scribes and Pharisees.

Instead, we are to seek ***"his righteousness."*** Now where can we find *"his righteousness"?* The answer is not in your righteousness or in mine, but *in Christ's!* ***The righteousness of God is in Christ!*** The righteousness of Jesus is God's righteousness! ***We are to seek Christ's righteousness, and it is found only through faith in his blood.*** Why the blood? Because:

The blood embodies and testifies to the finished work of Jesus Christ.

God's righteousness cannot be achieved by *"doing something,"* or by *doing greater or better works* than someone else. Neither can it be found in conforming to a certain standard of righteous living. This is what the legalist demands of himself, because this is what the law demands. The problem remains: *No one has ever been able to keep the law* except one, and He died on the cross to redeem us from the curse of the law (Gal. 3:13).

The curse of the law is not only death—the curse of the law is man's inability to keep or fulfill the demands of the law (Gal. 3:11-12).

When we examine the scriptures from Sinai, we are *unable* to see salvation through grace alone. We see something entirely different! *We see ourselves "doing something" to obtain and maintain righteousness with God.*

"Doing something" in order to obtain and maintain righteousness with God is the heart and soul of legalism!

We must now ask ourselves: *What did Christ mean when he said, "except your righteousness shall exceed the righteousness of the scribes and Pharisees, ye shall in no case enter into the kingdom of heaven"? There can be only one correct interpretation.*

Jesus wanted the multitude to know that the righteousness of the scribes and Pharisees was based on *righteousness through works*—on *legalism*! So then, how can we as grace believers exceed the righteousness of the scribes and Pharisees? By doing greater and better works? Ten thousand times—no! We exceed the righteousness of the scribes and Pharisees by receiving someone else's righteousness. That is:

We must have the righteousness of God imputed to us through faith in the finished work of Christ!

This righteousness comes to us when we believe on Jesus Christ as our savior. The Bible teaches us that:

For with the heart man believeth unto righteousness;
(Rom. 10:10)

This righteousness is *a gift of God's grace*, not the result of our works (Rom. 5:17). So:

While the legalist is working to establish his own righteousness and trusting in himself that he is righteous, the grace believer is walking with God and trusting in the shed blood of Christ that he is righteous (Rom. 10:3; Lk. 18:9).

Friend, if your salvation depends on what you do, you are a legalist and no better off than the Pharisees. According to the apostle Paul, *you have fallen from grace* (Gal. 5:4). It is just that simple.

However, if your salvation depends on what Christ did in your behalf, you are a grace believer. You are saved by *grace through faith*. Your righteous standing is in God's grace, not in your works (Rom. 5:2). It is just that simple.

Beholding His Glory

And it came to pass about an eight days after these sayings, he took Peter and John and James, and went up into a mountain to pray.

And as he prayed, the fashion of his countenance was altered, and his raiment was white and glistering.

And, behold, there talked with him two men, which were Moses and Elias:

Who appeared in glory, and spake of his decease which he should accomplish at Jerusalem.

(Lk. 9:28-31)

And there was a cloud that overshadowed them: and a voice came out of the cloud, saying, This is my beloved Son: hear him. And suddenly, when they had looked round about, they saw no man any more, save Jesus only with themselves.

(Mk. 9:7-8)

And the Word was made flesh, and dwelt among us, (and we beheld his glory, the glory as of the only begotten of the Father,) full of grace and truth.

(Jn. 1:14)

We have examined the ministry of legalism from the vantage point of Sinai, the ministry of grace from the vantage point of Calvary, and the nature and characteristics of each type of ministry.

There is another mountain between *Sinai* and *Calvary*. That mountain is known as *The Mount of Transfiguration*. It was there *Peter, James, and John witnessed a glorious revelation or unveiling of the glory and majesty of Christ.* John and Peter refer to the *Mount of Transfiguration* in their writings (Jn. 1:14; 2 Pet. 1:16-18). The transfiguration of Jesus had such a profound impact on them. Why? Was it simply for the Father to validate the deity of Christ?

I believe this event has far more significance than just to show Christ's deity. This indescribable event more than any other allowed the apostles to see a *type* of *the Old and New Covenants in transition* and a glimpse of the glory of each. On this holy mount:

- *Moses and Elijah—represented the Old Covenant*
- *Christ—represented the New Covenant*

Jesus is seen here talking with Moses and Elijah *in glory*. They are talking together about his death which he should accomplish at Jerusalem (Lk. 9:31). *I believe they were speaking of the atonement (the finished work of redemption) Jesus will provide to the world at Calvary.*

Why Moses and Elijah?

Moses *was the lawgiver* from Mt. Sinai. Elijah was the great *prophet* of Mt. Carmel. (Remember, it was Moses and Elijah to whom the Pharisees and James and John, the sons of thunder, appealed as the basis for dealing with the woman taken in adultery and the Samaritans earlier on).

Often in scripture *the Old Testament is referred to as* ***the law and the prophets*** (Matt. 7:12). *Moses and Elijah represent the Old Testament from Genesis through Malachi*—the covenant under which the law was in force. Dispensationally, *this covenant lasted from the giving of the law at Sinai until the death of Jesus at Calvary*. Moses and Elijah are seen here to be in agreement with the Father and Christ, and they *validated* Christ's death on the cross. Unknown to the apostles at this time is the revelation that:

The death of Jesus at Calvary would mark the end of the age of the law and usher in the church age or the dispensation of grace.

This is why *Christ forbade the disciples to speak of the event until after he rose again. For they did not yet understand the work of his atonement at Calvary nor his subsequent resurrection. These things were still a mystery to them* (Mk. 9:9-10). Suffice it to say it is not as important what was said on the mount, as it is what the apostles saw.

The End of an Age

What the apostles saw was a *foreshadow of the transition from the age of the law to the age of grace.* This transition was represented by Jesus, Moses and Elijah and the respective glory that accompanied them.

The chain of events is very significant. For what they witnessed was the glory of the law and the prophets being overshadowed by the glory of Christ. They witnessed *a type and shadow* of the end of one age or dispensation and the beginning of another. This age of *grace* was to be ushered in after Christ's death.

After Jesus was transfigured, Moses and Elijah appeared *in glory* (in a glorious manner) and spoke with Jesus. The apostles witnessed the glory that accompanied them. Moses and Elijah manifested and represented the lesser glory of the Old Testament. Paul, speaking of the glory of law and grace, said, **"that which was made glorious,** [the law] **had no glory in this respect, by reason of the glory that excelleth** [grace]." (2 Cor. 3:10). That helps us to understand that:

The glory of the law cannot be compared to the glory that is revealed in grace.

The glory that accompanied Christ was said to be *excellent* (2 Pet. 1:17). This was not said of the glory of Moses or Elijah. For Jesus is God in the flesh; He came in the glory he shared with his Father (Jn. 17:5). Such glory "that his face did shine as the sun, and his raiment was white as the light" (Matt 17:2).

From Glory to Glory

As grace believers, we must understand that in Christ we proceed from *glory to glory*, or from *law to grace*. We progress from *the ministry (ministration) of death* to *the ministry of the spirit, from the ministry of condemnation* to the *ministry of righteousness* (2 Cor. 3:7-10). This is what Paul means when he says we are changed from *glory to glory* (2 Cor. 3:18). He is talking about the law being replaced in our lives by the glory of grace and truth.

If we are to go from *glory to glory* or from law to grace, we must *reject and abandon legalism in all its forms* and embrace a pure ministry of grace and truth. Only then can we expect to see the glory of God manifest in our lives and in the lives of those whom we serve. The Holy Spirit is now saying to us:

If you want to see the great miracles of the last days, you must have a ministry of grace and truth, free from the yoke of legalism.

Just as John the Baptist prophesied, *"I must decrease but he must increase,"* now the apostles have a brilliant and shining example of this truth. The glory of one covenant was to be done away because of the glory of one more excellent (2 Cor. 3:11). Peter said,"We...were eye witnesses of his majesty" (2 Pet. 1:16). John said, "and we beheld his glory, the glory as of the only begotten of the Father, full of grace and truth" (Jn. 1:14). Paul, spoke of "the praise of the glory of his grace, wherein he hath made us accepted in the beloved" (Eph. 1:6).

Since my life and ministry have been transformed by *grace*, much of my theology and ministry have been transformed to embrace the redemption and *grace* that is in Christ Jesus. As with the earlier example of *Ishmael and Isaac*, I understand that:

Legalism is contrary to and cannot co-exist with the ministry of grace and truth.

Like the apostles, I no longer see Jesus in the crowd sharing glory with Moses and Elijah. In fact, I no longer see Moses or Elijah at all. For grace does not share any glory with the law. I now see Christ in his glory alone!

7

This Thing Called Grace

For by grace are ye saved through faith; and that not of yourselves: it is the gift of God: not of works, lest any man should boast.
(Eph. 2:8-9)

Before we examine *the Spirit of grace,* we must first define what *grace* is. *What is this thing called grace?* Moreover, *what exactly does it mean to be saved by grace?*

The Patented Definition of Grace

Some have said that grace simply means *favor*. That's a good start. Grace certainly includes favor, but, my friend, *the grace of God is much more than favor. Some have gone a little farther and have defined grace as un-deserved favor.* That is even better. *Grace certainly is not deserved.* However, to the believer in Christ Jesus there is more to grace than this.

I remember when I was a child in Sunday school. The teacher would ask the class, "What does the word *grace* mean*?* We all knew the traditional answer because we heard someone else say it us. Someone in the class would answer, "The unmerited favor of God." However, we could not explain what that really meant.

Today, when asked the same question, many still reply, *"why, the un-merited favor of God."* However, *saying t is one thing but understanding it and then believing it is quite another story.* Oftentimes we have spoken what we don't understand. Moreover, we have not truly believed what we thought we understood. *Being saved by grace is one of those "things" many talk about but don't truly understand or even believe.* Because, if we did, my brothers and sisters, *our lives would be different and so would our theology.* For instance:

How many times have you heard a preacher say, "We are saved by grace," and then add the disclaimer, "but you have to live right in order to make it in."

Does this sound familiar? Better yet, does this sound more than just a little bit strange? *To say that you are saved by grace, and then imply that you are really saved by works?* It does indeed sound strange if you are a true believer in salvation through God's grace alone. In my opinion, such preachers do not understand salvation by grace at all!

The Free Gift of God's Unmerited Favor

We have all heard *the patented definition of grace*. Frankly, I believe that it is a good one and a strong one. When I used to hear the definition of grace, it sounded so sterile, hollow, and abstract. I thought to myself, *"Is that it? Is that all it means?"* I often thought to myself, *"What does un-merited favor really mean? Surely, there must be a better way to define God's grace."*

After *forty-five* years of God's *unconditional* love and kindness toward me, I believe I now understand what *unmerited favor* is. I have seen and experienced it many times in my life. I can truly say, *"I am saved by grace and not by my works!"* Herein rests *the power and the simplicity of the gospel.*

A man or woman *(a sinner)* ***can be regenerated*** *(born again)* ***into the kingdom of God, and be eternally delivered from the presence, power, and penalty of sin. Moreover, he can be sealed and preserved unto eternal life. All this is made possible without that person's works*** *(righteous deeds or human merit)* ***taken into account*** (Tit. 3:5).

Why? Because:

Salvation is by God's grace—the free gift of His unmerited favor alone. Moreover, it is through faith in the blood of Jesus Christ alone!

Yes, we need to know that God's grace is His favor. Yes, we need to know that God's grace is undeserved. Yes, we need to know that God's grace is without *"merit," meaning, we have and can do nothing to earn it or deserve it in any sense.* However, most importantly we need to know that *God's grace is* ***free.*** *It costs us nothing.*

It is through grace that God expresses His kindness toward us through Christ Jesus (Eph. 2:7).

It really is *amazing grace*, and it really is just that simple! Paul tells us: The grace of God is also *the grace of our Lord Jesus Christ*!

For ye know the grace of our Lord Jesus Christ, that, though he was rich, yet for your sakes he became poor, that ye through his poverty might be rich.

(2 Cor. 8:9)

You see, the grace of God that *bringeth salvation* is given to us through our Lord and Savior, Jesus Christ (Tit. 2:11).

The means of this grace is the infinite, eternal love of God and the offering of the body of Jesus Christ once for all (Heb. 10:10).

This grace was *motivated by God's love* for man (Jn. 3:16; 1 Jn. 3:16) and provides God's *redemptive remedy* for sin through the blood of Jesus. Furthermore, this grace also provides *the power* to overcome *sin, the flesh, the world, and the devil* through the indwelling *Holy Spirit*. Hear it again:

Grace not only provides the remedy for sin. It also provides and imparts the means to overcome sin.

That is why Paul could say, *"where sin abounded, grace did much more abound"* (Rom. 5:20). God's answer to man's sin was to provide grace that would abound beyond all of our sin. Where did so great salvation come from? Paul says that God's grace brought this salvation.

Never underestimate the power of grace to transform a person's life.

Because many preachers *do not* understand the power of the *grace* of God to change a believer's life, they have scoffed at the idea that:

Grace is more powerful than the law in dealing with sin in the lives of believers. You see, the law seeks to reform man from the outside, but grace seeks to transform a man from the inside (Heb. 8:10).

Another example of this is the healing of *the impotent man* at the pool of *Bethesda*. After the man was healed, Jesus found him again in the temple a changed man. What changed this man so much that he was now a worshiper of God? It was *the work of grace* in the man's heart. Jesus gave the man a word of *grace and truth*:

"Behold, thou art made whole: sin no more, lest a worse thing come unto thee" (Jn. 5:14). The world needs able ministers of the New Testament who can minister in *grace and truth* (2 Cor. 3:6). Christ gave us this model for New Testament ministry.

The Spirit of Grace

The Spirit of the Lord GOD is upon me; because the LORD hath anointed me to preach good tidings unto the meek; he hath sent me to bind up the brokenhearted, to proclaim liberty to the captives, and the opening of the prison to them that are bound;

To proclaim the acceptable year of the LORD, and the day of vengeance of our God; to comfort all that mourn;

(Isa. 61:1-2)

THE SPIRIT OF THE LORD IS UPON ME, BECAUSE HE HATH ANOINTED ME TO PREACH THE GOSPEL TO THE

POOR; HE HATH SENT ME TO HEAL THE BROKENHEARTED, TO PREACH DELIVERANCE TO THE CAPTIVES, AND RECOVERING OF SIGHT TO THE BLIND, TO SET AT LIBERTY THEM THAT ARE BRUISED,

TO PREACH THE ACCEPTABLE YEAR OF THE LORD.

And he began to say unto them, This day is this scripture fulfilled in your ears.

And all bare him witness, and wondered at the gracious words which proceeded out of his mouth....

(Lk. 4:18-19, 21-22, emphasis added)

Now that we have defined grace as *the free gift of God's unmerited favor,* let us now define *the Spirit of grace.*

What Is the Spirit of Grace?

The Spirit of grace is the redemptive spirit or heart of God that is moved with unmerited favor and good will toward man in redemption (Lk. 2:14).

The *Spirit of grace* is mentioned specifically in *Hebrews 10:29 and Zechariah 12:10.* The *Spirit of grace* is freely given to the church today and it will be *poured out* upon the *house of Israel* during the *millennium,* the *one thousand year reign* of Christ on the earth.

What Does the Spirit of Grace Do?

The Spirit of grace creates the climate whereby grace and truth work together to bring salvation and its attending blessings to man.

Jesus Christ was *anointed with* the *Spirit of grace.* The *Spirit of grace* motivated his entire earthly ministry. It is the *Spirit of grace* that James and John lacked in their early ministry.

It is my opinion that *God desires every New Testament believer to manifest the Spirit of grace as we proceed to do ministry in Christ's name.* It is *the Spirit of grace* that the Pharisees lacked in

Christ's day. Moreover, it is the *Spirit of grace* that is lacking in the ministry of the legalist today. In essence:

It is the Spirit of grace that manifests the compassion, favor, and mercy of Jesus Christ.

The Spirit of grace is the true nature and spirit of Jesus Christ. As the ministry of grace and truth characterized the ministry of Jesus Christ,

The Spirit of grace also characterizes the true ministry of the end- time church and of the millennial kingdom. As the ministry of grace is restored to the church, we will see a phenomenal increase in the love, unity, and effectiveness of the Body of Christ.

Because of this, as in the end of the *cold war*, denominational barriers of self-righteousness will vanish, and walls of legalistic doctrine will be dismantled and carried away as rubbish. We will then see the outstanding signs and wonders for which we have waited.

Christ, The Anointed One

Jesus is *the Christ* or *anointed one*. His anointing and ministry is characterized in Isaiah 61 and Luke 4. His ministry is a ministry of grace and truth. He is anointed:

Isaiah 61	**Luke 4**
To preach good tidings,	*to preach the gospel*
To bind up the broken hearted	*to heal the broken hearted*
To proclaim liberty to the captives	*to preach deliverance to the captives*
	the recovering of sight to the blind,

Opening of the prison to them that are bound bruised,	*to set at liberty them that are*
To proclaim the acceptable year of the LORD, and the day of vengeance	*to preach ..acceptable year of the LORD,*
To comfort all that mourn in Zion.	

When we compare the *Messianic signs* of Luke 4:18-19, 21-22 and Isaiah 61:1-2, we find that they are somewhat different. In fact, some prophecies appear to be missing while other prophecies are referred to from other portions of Isaiah's book! Why is this so? We must understand that:

Prophecies concerning the work of the Messiah run throughout the book of Isaiah, and *some kingdom signs were present in Christ's earthly ministry, but not all* (Isa. 35,40,49,61).

There is a reason for this. There is approximately *a 2,000-year gap* of time between Christ's *First and Second Coming*. This explains why Christ quoted only certain scriptures from Isaiah and then said, *"This day is this scripture fulfilled in your ears."*

Christ did not mean that *all* the prophecies concerning him were fulfilled at that time. What did He mean? He was simply letting them know that the Messiah had arrived and *begun* his work. The Jews, of course, did not understand the gap of time between his First and Second Coming.

Christ's ministry *began* to be fulfilled while he was on earth. Luke, the author of the third gospel and the book of Acts writes,

[These things Jesus] "began both to do and teach until the day in which he was taken up," (Acts 1:2)

Since that time, ***Christ is continuing his ministry of grace and truth through the church today.*** You see, during Christ's earthly ministry *the people received just a 3 1/2-year glance at the* *promised* ***kingdom signs*** *of the millennium.* ***During the millennial reign of Christ as King, these signs will be seen for 1,000 years.*** Some of the kingdom signs that were present in Christ's ministry are found in Isaiah chapter 35.

Then the eyes of the blind shall be opened, and the ears of the deaf shall be unstopped.

Then shall the lame man leap as an hart, and the tongue of the dumb sing...

(Isa. 35:5-6)

Though Christ fulfilled only certain prophecies at *his First Advent, the Messianic prophecies pertain to both:*

- *His pre-millennial earthly ministry* (*His First Advent*), *and*

- *His millennial kingdom ministry* (*His Second Advent*)

During the ***Kingdom Age,*** Christ will finish the work he *began* to do at his *First Coming*. Meanwhile, Christ is presently continuing his ministry through New Testament believers today. This is part of *the mystery* of God spoken of by the Apostles that was "hid from ages and from generations, but now is made manifest to his saints" (Col. 1:26-27; Eph. 3:2-6).

This will help explain *why* Jesus was rejected and crucified by the Jews at His *First Coming*. They *did not* understand that He came to establish *a spiritual kingdom* (the church) at His First Coming, and will establish *a literal kingdom* at His *Second Coming* (2 Tim. 4:1). He was therefore rejected as king of the Jews and crucified when He failed to establish His earthly kingdom immediately (Lk. 19:11).

Art Thou He That Should Come?

The *hidden mystery of the church age* [dispensation] caused some confusion even among Christ's followers as to His claim to be the Messiah (Acts 1:6-7). An example of this is the inquiry of

John the Baptist.

Now when John had heard in the prison the works of Christ, he sent two of his disciples,

And said unto him, Art thou he that should come, or do we look for another?

Jesus answered and said unto them, Go and shew John again those things which ye do hear and see:

The blind receive their sight, and the lame walk, the lepers are cleansed, and the deaf hear, the dead are raised up, and the poor have the gospel preached to them.

And blessed is he, whosoever shall not be offended in me.

(Matt. 11:2-6)

Not even *John the Baptist* understood the *gap* of time between Christ's *First and Second Coming*. He who had seen the Spirit like a dove descend and heard the Father's voice from heaven began to *doubt* Christ's claim to be the Messiah. Why? John was cast into prison and sentenced to death because he had proclaimed the Word of God. Sometime afterward John was perplexed as to *why he was not yet set free by Christ.*

John knew the scriptures foretold that the Messiah would come "to proclaim liberty to the captives, and the opening of the prison to them that are bound" (Isa. 61:1). Yet, no one had come to set him free! John the Baptist was left in prison to be beheaded. Therefore, he sent two of his disciples to ask Jesus,

"Art thou he that should come, or do we look for another?"
(Matt. 11:3)

His own cousin whom he had validated and declared to be the Christ did not come to save him! Jesus allowed his cousin John to languish in prison. Why? Because *John did not understand one aspect of Christ's ministry.*

The *opening of the prison to them that are bound will be performed at Christ's Second Advent!* ***During his First Advent, he released none from prison!*** *It is during the Second Advent that Christ will fulfill the remaining signs and prophecies concerning* *him.* These include:

To open the blind eyes, to bring out the prisoners from the prison, and them that sit in darkness out of the prison house.

(Isa. 42:7)

That thou mayest say to the prisoners, Go forth; to them that are in darkness, Shew yourselves...

(Isa. 49:9)

It is then that He will *comfort those that mourn in Zion, to give them beauty for ashes, the oil of joy for mourning, and the garment of praise for the spirit of heaviness* (Isa. 61:3).

The Spirit of grace is yet fulfilling the remaining portions of Isaiah's prophecy concerning the work and ministry of the Messiah. We now live in the *day of salvation*. This day of salvation is also *the acceptable year of the Lord* where Jew and Gentile can be saved. This is the *church age*. This is the promise of the dispensation or *of the day of grace* (Isa. 40:6-13; 2 Cor. 6:2).

And these signs shall follow them that believe; In my name shall they ...

(Mk. 16:17)

Every New Testament believer is an extension of Christ's ministry. Christ performs his ministry through us. What we do, we do in the name of Jesus! That is why the apostle Peter could say, "Jesus Christ maketh thee whole" (Acts 9:34). Also, "..and that signs and wonders may be done by the name of thy holy child Jesus" (Acts 4:30). We are performing ministry in *the name* of Jesus or *in his stead.*

With this understanding let us take care to manifest the *Spirit of grace* and guard our hearts against the dangers of legalism.

PART II

JUSTIFICATION
&
THE STANDING OF THE BELIEVER

Justification:

That act of God
wherein
the believer in Christ Jesus,
through grace,
is justified freely from all things,
and is declared righteous,
and in right standing
with God the Father,
without regard to any works
or merit
on the part of the believer in Christ.

8

<u>*Faith vs. Works*</u>

Was not Abraham our father justified by works when he had offered up Isaac his son upon the altar?

Seest thou how faith wrought with his works, and by works was faith made perfect?

And the scripture was fulfilled which saith, Abraham believed God, and it was imputed unto him for righteousness: and he was called the Friend of God.

(Jas. 2:21-23)

For if Abraham were justified by works, he hath whereof to glory; but not before God.

For what saith the scripture? ABRAHAM BELIEVED GOD, AND IT WAS COUNTED UNTO HIM FOR RIGHTEOUSNESS.

Now to him that worketh is the reward not reckoned of grace, but of debt.

But to him that worketh not, but believeth on him that justifieth the ungodly, his faith is counted for righteousness.

(Rom. 4:2-5 emphasis added)

The Fall

At the moment of *the Fall*, Adam became *a transgressor—a sinner.* When Adam fell through transgression, he *forfeited* his *right to the tree of life*. He died *spiritually*, and his *relationship to God* was *changed* to that of a *sinner*. Adam was unable to fellowship openly with God as before (Gen. 3:22-24; Rev. 22:14). Because

Adam was the Federal (representative) head of the human race,

Adam's transgression changed man's moral standing and man's relationship to God (Rom. 5:17-19).

Man became *a sinner*. He became one of the *"fallen ones"* with the knowledge of good and evil (obedience and disobedience). *Prior to this time, only the fallen angels had the knowledge of good and evil.* Before the fall, man had only the knowledge of good.

Man lost at least two things during the Fall. One was *eternal life*. The other was *sovereignty and dominion over the earth.* These rights were kept in *abeyance* or *suspended* until God through Christ could restore them to man. *Since man legally lost them to Satan, man had to legally reclaim* them (Rom. 5:19).

The Declaration of Righteousness

The incarnation was God's *remedy* for man's plight (Gen. 3:15). *God took upon Himself the nature of man in the person of Jesus Christ.* God came into this world as *a man* to redeem mankind from *the curse of the law, sin, and death.* Through the atonement, Jesus will ultimately *restore* man to his original spiritual state and purpose.

Redemption: *That remedial act or process of God whereby God through the atoning death of His Son,* ***purchases,*** *or* ***buys back from Satan all rights that man forfeited or lost in the Fall.*** *Thus, restoring man's* ***right*** *to sovereignty and dominion over the earth, as well as his right to the tree of eternal life* (Rev. 22:14).

Regeneration: *That act or process of God in* ***which the spirit of man is regenerated, or born again,*** *and* ***fellowship is restored*** *with the Spirit of God.*

There are at least four *redemptive processes* that occur when the believer is regenerated. At the moment of regeneration and salvation the believer is also:

- ***Justified:*** *Declared righteous in Christ* (Rom. 8:30)
- ***Sanctified***: *Set apart in Christ* (Heb. 10:29)
- ***Adopted:*** *Made a legal heir in Christ* (Gal.4:5; Eph. 1:5)
- ***Sealed:*** *Preserved in Christ* (Eph. 1:13, 4:30;1 Thess. 5:23; Jude 1)

Justification: *That act or process of God whereby God* ***declares*** *a man* ***righteous or in right moral and legal standing*** *with himself.*

When a man is justified, he is declared legally moral and spiritually right or righteous in the sight of God. Justification involves *the process* of the *imputation* and the *declaration* of righteousness. However:

Righteousness must first be imputed before one can be declared righteous or justified.

The question remains, "Is the process of justification by faith or by works?"

The Contradiction?

In reading the above referenced scriptures, *it seems that Paul and James are in contradiction with each other* as to whether Abraham was justified by *works* or by *faith.* While James *includes* faith as part of that process, he also says that works made Abraham's faith *perfect* (finished or complete).

Paul asserts that faith alone justified Abraham and that works had no part whatsoever in Abraham's justification.

We shall now attempt to reconcile these two points of view. This is very important because the legalist has sought *refuge* in the words of James and his assertion of justification by works. It is my belief that:

Justification is based solely on the merit of the finished work of Christ and has nothing whatsoever to do with the meritorious

works of the one justified.

Substitution and Atonement

In order to understand the doctrine of justification and James' use of Abraham and Isaac, *we must take into account two underlying principles.* These are the principles of *Substitution and Atonement.* We shall attempt to demonstrate that:

These underlying principles are not the foundation of justification by works, but they are the very foundation of justification by faith.

1) <u>The Principle of Substitution</u> declares that *Christ died for us*, and *He died in our place. He who knew no sin became sin*, and He *became an offering or sacrifice* for sin.

As *the ram* was *substituted* or killed in the stead of Isaac, Christ was a *vicarious substitute* for us at Calvary. Calvary was the *altar and place of propitiation* from which *Christ took upon Himself our sin* and paid the *ransom of His blood* to redeem us from the curse of sin (1 Cor. 6:20; 2 Cor. 5: 21).

2) <u>The Principle of Atonement</u> declares that *Christ through the shedding of his sinless and innocent blood, purged, cleansed, and removed from us our sins,* thereby giving us *life.*

Without the *shedding of blood* there is *no remission of sins* (Heb. 9:22). Christ is the *propitiation* (mercy seat or sacrifice of atonement) that causes us to draw "*prope*" (near) to God. Through His atoning death, God's wrath is *appeased* and we are now *reconciled* to God and can now say there is ***at-one-ment,*** or agreement between God and man (Lev. 17:11).

The principles of substitution and atonement are the heart and essence of grace theology.

If we understand the principles of substitution and atonement, we must also understand that:

The legalist's doctrine of righteousness through works based

on human merit is incompatible with the principles of substitution and atonement and therefore must be rejected.

The Bible says plainly:

For if Abraham were justified by works, he hath whereof to glory; but not before God.
(Rom. 4:2).

New Testament salvation is founded on *principles* that were introduced early in man's history. *The principles of substitution and atonement were first set in motion in the Garden of Eden* and are consistent only with being saved by God's grace through faith alone. Furthermore, *these principles can be seen in every age or dispensation from Eden to Calvary. It is upon these principles that every blood sacrifice offered unto God is based throughout scripture,* including James' reference to the offering of Isaac.

Is it not strange that James would use a most powerful *example of substitution and atonement* and then declare that Abraham was *justified by works when he had offered up Isaac*? I concur with James. What better example of being justified by faith is there than the offering of Isaac? Here is why I believe this is so.

The Offering of Isaac

- *Revealed and confirmed* (in type) *the finished work of God in Christ at Calvary.*

- *Revealed and confirmed the principles of substitution and atonement.*

- *Revealed and confirmed to Abraham that his standing with God (his justification) was predicated solely on a vicarious sacrifice of substitution and atonement and not on his obedience (works).*

Because of this *evidence* or *proof* of ***faith*** in God's promises (the offering of Isaac), James declares Abraham was called *the* *friend of God* (Isa. 41:8).

The Imputation of Righteousness

Why does the scriptures say Abraham ***believed*** (or trusted) God, and it was *imputed* (Rom. 4:22), *accounted* (Gal. 3:6), or *reckoned* (Rom. 4:9) unto him *for righteousness?* Do these terms sound familiar? *These terms are bookkeeping and accounting terms, as of an accountant's ledger of accounts.* Here we are given *a word picture* of **righteousness being given to Abraham's account** or in Abraham's behalf. The question I have for the legalist is:

If works justified Abraham, why did he need righteousness to be given in his behalf, since his own works of obedience should have been sufficient to justify him?

Furthermore, *whose righteousness was imputed to Abraham's account,* since his righteousness alone *was not considered* part of the equation of righteousness and justification by faith? We all know the answer. The righteousness *imputed* to Abraham was the righteousness of God in Christ (Rom. 3:22; 1 Cor. 1:30; 2 Cor. 5:21). This was absolutely *necessary* under the principles of *substitution and atonement.*

The offering of Jesus Christ balanced the books of the believer's debt of righteousness. Moreover, because of Calvary, Christ's righteousness is now imputed to the believer's account. This is how a believer becomes justified before God. The process of the imputation of righteousness is by faith alone.

The Key to Understanding Faith and Works

The *key to understanding* whether justification is by faith or by works can be found in answering:

Two Important Questions:

1*) Was Abraham justified by works* **because** *he offered his son* *in obedience to God? Or,*

2) Was Abraham's obedience in offering his son evidence that he was ***already*** *justified by faith* ***before*** *he offered Isaac?*

In other words, we must first ascertain—W*hen was Abraham justified? Was it* **before, during, or after** *he offered up Isaac?* I believe this is *the* ***key*** *to understanding the seeming contradiction between the words of Paul and the words of James. Furthermore, this is the key to understanding the place of faith and works in the life of the believer.*

And the scripture was fulfilled which saith, Abraham believed God, and it was imputed unto him for righteousness: and he was called the Friend of God.

(Jas. 2:21-23)

For what saith the scripture? ABRAHAM BELIEVED GOD, AND IT WAS COUNTED UNTO HIM FOR RIGHTEOUSNESS.

(Rom. 4:3, emphasis added)

What did Abraham believe? When did Abraham believe it? In addition, what was imputed to him for righteousness? The answer can again be found in the method or vantage point of interpretation.

Justification and Sinai

The legalist believes that Abraham's *works of obedience* resulted in his justification. When the legalist interprets these verses from *the vantage point of Sinai*, he reasons that Abraham was justified by works *because* he offered his son in ***obedience*** to God. In other words,

The legalist believes Abraham offered up his son in order to obtain righteousness (justification).

Justification and Calvary

The grace believer believes that Abraham's works were the *result of his prior justification* by faith. When the grace believer interprets these verses from *the vantage point of Calvary,* he understands that *Abraham's obedience in offering his son was evidence that he was already justified by faith.* In other words,

The grace believer believes Abraham offered up his son because he was already declared righteous (justified).

A careful look at the Genesis record of the life of Abraham reveals that:

Abraham was already justified by faith before he even received the command to offer Isaac. In fact:

Abraham was justified by faith before Isaac was born!

If this were true, *would this not shatter the legalist's interpretation of these verses?* Then why does James make the plain statement that "Abraham our father was justified by works, when he had offered Isaac his son upon the altar" (Jas. 2:21). I believe James uses Abraham and Isaac to illustrate that:

Abraham's obedience in offering Isaac was evidence (or proof) that Abraham was already justified by faith before he offered Isaac. Abraham was not justified as a result of offering Isaac in obedience to God.

You see, *Abraham was well acquainted with the principles of substitution and atonement at* the time he had offered Isaac. He had offered many sacrifices to God prior to the offering of Isaac. However, when Abraham offered the ram *in the stead of his son* (Gen. 22:13), he was giving his descendants *a figure, or a type of Christ being offered by the Father in the behalf of mankind* (Heb. 11:19). I believe *Abraham knew by faith* exactly what God was planning to do (Heb. 11:17).

How do we know this? *Abraham himself provides the clue.* On the way to Moriah, Abraham leaves his servants with the donkeys and then reassures Isaac by saying,

My son, God will provide himself a lamb for a burnt offering:
(Gen. 22:8)

How did Abraham know this? *He looked through the eyes of faith.* Whereas God spared Abraham's son, God did not spare his own son, but "delivered him up for us all" (Rom. 8:32).

Even God would not violate the principles of substitution and atonement set in motion in the Garden of Eden. As *God sacrificed the lamb in the garden* (a life for a life) and as *Abraham sacrificed a ram at Moriah* (a life for a life), even so did *the Father sacrifice his Son at Calvary* (a life for a life), that he might redeem man from the *curse* of the law, sin, and death (Gal. 3:13).

Through the offering of Isaac, God gave to man a perfect *illustration* of the *unconditional redemptive love* he has for mankind, even to the extent of offering His only begotten Son.

Christ therefore became the true substitute and sacrifice of atonement (propitiation) *for our sins*
(1 Jn. 2:2).

By Faith Abraham

By faith Abraham, when he was tried, offered up Isaac: and he that had received the promises offered up his only begotten son,
(Heb. 11:17)

How did Abraham offer up Isaac? The writer of Hebrews says that Abraham offered up Isaac by *faith.* Paul tells us that "faith cometh by hearing, and hearing by the word of God" (Rom. 10:17). God's word of faith came to Abraham in the form of *a promise.* This promise was the *bedrock* upon which Abraham established his relationship with God. The writer of Hebrews also says that *he that had received the promises offered up his only begotten son.* Among those promises was one that said:

... This shall not be thine heir; but he that shall come forth out of thine own bowels shall be thine heir. And he brought him forth abroad, and said, Look now toward heaven, and tell the stars, if thou be able to number them: and he said unto him, So shall thy seed be. ***And he believed in the LORD; and he counted it to him for righteousness.***

(Gen. 15:4-6, emphasis added)

There it is! This is the point *in time* where God declares that Abraham was justified! This is *what* Abraham believed! This is *when* Abraham believed! Moreover, this is *where*:

God declares that righteousness was imputed to Abraham on the basis of his faith in the promises of God alone.

Abraham's justification had *nothing whatsoever* to do with *Abraham's works* of obedience! It would be another ***fifteen years*** before Isaac would be born. Then another ***seventeen years*** before God commanded him to offer Isaac. Yet, we find:

Abraham is already justified and declared righteous approximately thirty-two years before he offered Isaac on Mt. Moriah!

So when reconciling James and Paul we must first understand that,

Abraham offered Isaac because he was already justified (declared righteous), rather than to obtain justification.

Faith, Justification, And Works

James *could not* have meant that *Abraham was justified as a result of offering Isaac.* I believe James was sharing with us another very important principle. That is, *in relation to faith, justification, and works,*

Works are only important in the context that works are evidence of the faith that already exists in one already justified.

In other words—***faith precedes*** and does *not* follow works, and ***works follow*** *justification. The proper sequence of events is:*

Faith ⟶ ***Justification*** ⟶ ***Works***

Abraham's faith *preceded* his justification and his justification *preceded* his works. The scriptural record will support no other conclusion.

The Seal of the Covenant

To further illustrate the truth that *faith precedes justification and that justification precedes works,* let us consider for a moment:

- *The Old Testament ordinance of* **circumcision**
- *The New Testament ordinance of* **water baptism**

Both were commanded of God.

- *One was given to Israel through Abraham* (Gen. 17:10 - 11).
- *One was given to the church through Christ* (Mk. 16:15 - 16).

- *One is the Old Testament type.*
- *One is the New Testament antitype* or *fulfillment of the type* (Col. 2:11 - 12).

Paul explains in the book of Romans, the ordinance of circumcision was a ***sign,*** or ***seal,*** *of the righteousness of the faith which he* (Abraham) **had being yet uncircumcised** (before he was circumcised) (Rom. 4:6-13). Why?

... that he might be the father of all them that believe, though they be not circumcised; that righteousness might be imputed unto them also.

(Rom. 4:11)

Notice carefully that,

Circumcision did not justify Abraham or give him righteousness.

It (circumcision) was a *testimony* or *a sign* of the *imputed righteousness* Abraham had already received by *faith in the promises of God.* These promises were ratified and established in a covenant of blood. Circumcision was *a sign* or *seal* of the blood covenant God made with Abraham (Gen. 15:8-18, 17:7-14). Yet:

Abraham's faith and his justification preceded or occurred prior to the ordinance of circumcision. Likewise,

Circumcision is a type of the New Testament ordinance of water baptism (Col. 2:11-12). As in the case of circumcision:

- *Water baptism* **does not** *justify the believer or give him righteousness.*
- *Water baptism is a* **sign** *or seal of the righteousness the believer has* ***already received by faith alone.***
- *Water baptism is* ***only*** *for the believer who has* ***already*** *been justified by faith alone* (Mk. 16:16).

In relation to faith, water baptism is only important in the following context:

Water baptism is an evidence or outward sign of the faith and of the covenant that already exists between Christ and one already saved or justified.

Therefore we must conclude that *one is baptized because he is already saved* (justified) *and not in order to be saved.* Yet, some in the Body of Christ have it backwards. All grace believers understand this principle. The principle of justification by faith and the harmony of scripture will support nothing else.

The Test Of Mark 16:16

He that believeth and is baptized shall be saved; but he that believeth not shall be damned.

(Mk. 16:16)

Some may ask, "Well, what about *Mark 16:16*?" *Have you ever wondered why water baptism is mentioned in the first half of the verse and yet there is no mention of water baptism in the last part of this verse?* Here's why:

The test of Mark 16:16 is not the essentiality of water baptism, but the essentiality of *faith in the gospel.*

What is the Gospel?

The gospel is the good news of the ***finished work*** *of the death, burial, and resurrection of Jesus Christ* (1 Cor. 15:1-4)!

What we need to understand here is:

It is the absence of faith in the gospel that will ultimately condemn the lost soul—not the absence of water baptism. *He that believeth not* (baptized or not) *shall be damned!* To emphasize the truth on this point, one need only consider *that:*

If one is baptized but does not have faith in the gospel (the blood atonement and finished work of Calvary), he will still be lost.

Some legalists, however, greatly err regarding baptism because *they do not understand the principle of justification by faith in the blood of Jesus alone.*

For many years, as a *legalist* I could not see the light concerning water baptism. My understanding was *impaired* because I approached these scriptures from the *vantage point* of Sinai and not from Calvary. A veil of legalism covered my eyes from the truth.

Only by rightly dividing the scriptures and applying the principle of justification by faith do I now understand the truth. That is:

The emphasis of Mark 16:16 is not on the importance of baptism to be saved, but on the importance of faith in the gospel to be saved.

Justified By Faith

Calvary is the place where the New Testament was ratified in a covenant of blood—the blood of Jesus Christ, the *Lamb of God* (Jn. 1:29).

As the believer is justified by faith before he is baptized— Likewise,

Abraham was justified by faith in Genesis chapter 15 (Gen. 15:1-6), ***at least thirty-two years before he offered Isaac in Genesis chapter 22.*** The offering of Isaac was ***a testimony, a witness, or good report*** that ***Abraham believed in the promises of God and was already justified by faith*** (Gen. 15:6).

Abraham heard the word of God and *the obedience of faith* took him to the land of Moriah where he offered Isaac (Rom. 16:26; Gen. 22:18; Heb. 11:8). Abraham offered up *Isaac taking into account* the promises that God had already made before concerning him. That promise was:

And God said, Sarah thy wife shall bear thee a son indeed; and thou shalt call his name Isaac: And I will establish my covenant with him for an everlasting covenant, and with his seed after him.

But my covenant will I establish with Isaac, which Sarah shall bear unto thee at this set time next year.

(Gen. 17:19, 21)

The writer of Hebrews tells us that *by faith Abraham* ... ***offered up Isaac.*** He did not say Abraham almost offered Isaac. He says "*he who had received the promises* (plural) ***offered up*** *his only begotten son*, of whom it was said, That in Isaac shall thy seed be called. ***Accounting*** *that God was able to raise him up, even from* *the dead; from which also he received him in a figure"* (Heb. 11:17-19 emphasis added).

In the eternal mind of God, by offering Isaac, Abraham had fulfilled all of God's Word. *Abraham offered Isaac in faith.* Isn't it interesting that the writer of Hebrews calls Isaac Abraham's ***only begotten son***, although Ishmael, Abraham's other son, was still alive? Why? I believe:

Abraham believed that God would have to raise Isaac from the dead if he shed the blood of Isaac, in order for God to bring to pass the promises He had made to Abraham. This means that:

Abraham knew by faith that God's promises to him could only be fulfilled in Isaac.

The offering of Isaac *demonstrated and confirmed* that Abraham was *already* justified by faith. So it is written that Abraham *became the father of all them that believe* (Rom. 4:11). Because, *through Abraham and the promises given to him by God, the believer has access by faith into this grace wherein he stands* (Rom. 5:2). For it is written, *"THE JUST SHALL LIVE BY FAITH"* (Rom. 1:17; Hab. 2:4 emphasis added).

What Shall We Say Then?

What shall we say then that Abraham our father, as pertaining to the flesh, hath found?

(Rom. 4:1)

At some point in Abraham's life, he *discovered* something about a righteous man's *standing* with God? What did he discover or find out? *Did he discover that he was justified by his works? Or rather, did he discover that he was justified by faith in the promises of God?* Paul taught us that:

Abraham found out two things.

- *A man* ***can have*** *righteousness* ***apart*** *from works.*

- *A man* ***cannot have*** *righteousness* ***apart*** *from faith in the promises of God.*

Paul understood *the* ***principle*** *of justification by faith alone* and therefore ***ties these promises made to Abraham to faith in the finished work of Christ alone.***

But now the righteousness of God without the law is manifested, being witnessed by the law and the prophets; even the righteousness of God which is by faith of Jesus Christ unto all and upon all them that believe...

(Rom. 3:21-22)

For Christ is the end of the law for righteousness to every one that believeth.

(Rom. 10:4)

...And by him all that believe are justified from all things, from which ye could not be justified by the law of Moses.

(Acts 13:39)

Therefore we conclude that a man is justified by faith without the deeds of the law.

(Rom. 3:28)

The believer's works of righteousness are not part of the justification process.

Paul confirms this to *Titus* when he writes:

Not by works of righteousness **which we have done,** *but according to his mercy he saved us, by the washing of regeneration, and renewing of the Holy Ghost;*

(Tit. 3:5 emphasis added)

Does the legalist really understand the consequence of what Paul just said? I think not. *Paul readily admits that we have done works of righteousness.* However, Paul stresses that these works *are not* the basis of our salvation. The basis of our salvation is God's mercy as experienced in the new birth. Let's look at it another way. Let's use the language of *mathematics* to express salvation through grace as an algebra equation.

The Grace Equation

The grace equation is an algebra formula based on Paul's letter to the Ephesians (Eph. 2:8-9). The formula helps one to understand the place of faith and works in the salvation process. The Ephesian formula when properly understood gives more meaning to the verses in Romans which declare:

For if Abraham were justified by works, he hath whereof to glory; but not before God.

(Rom. 4:2)

"Where is boasting then? It is excluded. By what law. Of works? Nay: but by the law of faith" (Rom. 3:27). Let's look at the formula.

For by grace are ye saved through faith; and that not of yourselves: it is the gift of God: not of works, lest any man should boast.

(Eph. 2:8-9)

(GRACE X GIFT OF FAITH) - WORKS = SALVATION
(10 X 10) - 0 = 100%

(GRACE X GIFT OF FAITH) X WORKS = NO SALVATION
(10 X 10) X 0 = 0%

A law is *a principle. The law* (or principle) *of works* allows one *to boast in his own works of self-righteousness.* However, *the law* (or principle) *of righteousness through faith does not.* Why? Because:

That which is of faith is rooted and grounded in the finished work of Jesus Christ and not in the works of the one justified.

So, it is written, "He that glorieth [boasteth] let him glory [boast] in the Lord" (1 Cor. 1:31). You see,

God (In His wisdom) ***realized that the only way to exclude man's boasting is to exclude the believer's works of righteousness from the process of salvation altogether.***

This is entirely what salvation by grace is all about!

It is the finished work of Christ through which the believer is justified!

There *is nothing* one can add to the cross of Calvary. *The Lord Jesus Christ has done and finished all the works necessary to justify the believer, now and forever more. His righteousness* as ***a gift*** is *imputed* to the believer (Rom. 5:15).

The moment he or she is born again, the believer is also justified. Once the believer is justified, he or she is declared righteous and in perfect legal and moral standing with God.

Abraham's faith was in *God's promise* to him—not in his works of obedience. Thus, he was justified by faith. So, what did James mean when he said Abraham was justified by works? Where do works come in? Moreover, why does James emphasize works in relation to faith?

9

<u>*Faith, Works, And Faith-Works*</u>

Even so faith, if it hath not works, is dead, being alone. Yea, a man may say, Thou hast faith, and I have works: shew me thy faith without thy works, and I will shew thee my faith by my works.

Seest thou how faith wrought with his works, and by works was faith made perfect?

For as the body without the spirit is dead, so faith without works is dead also.

(Jas. 2:17-18,22,26)

The Principle of Living Faith

James introduces us to another very important principle—the *principle of living faith.* What is living faith?

Living faith is faith that can be seen or evidenced in the life of the believer.

It is this characteristic of faith (that it can be seen) *that justifies a man* **before other men** *as to whether one truly has faith.* God sees and rewards faith (Heb. 11:6). An example of living faith is found in Luke's gospel.

And, behold, men brought in a bed a man which was taken with a palsy: and they sought means to bring him in, and to lay him before him. And when they could not find by what way they might bring him in because of the multitude, they went upon the housetop, and let him down through the tiling with his couch into the midst before Jesus. ***And when he saw their faith,*** *he said unto him, Man, thy sins are forgiven thee.*

(Lk. 5:18-20 emphasis added)

Show Me Thy Faith

While we must contend Abraham was not justified by works before God, it is also reasonable to assert *that works caused Abraham to* ***appear*** *justified before man and* ***validated*** *his faith before the eyes of his servants who accompanied him* to Mt. Moriah (Gen. 22:5). So, when James says,“ a man may say... show me thy faith” (Jas. 2:18). He is declaring,

The only way faith can be witnessed or seen by others is through a corresponding action on the part of the believer.

This is what is meant by the principle of living faith. ***Living faith is faith that can be seen.***

Two Kinds of Faith

James also reminds us that ***faith exists in two states of being—living faith and dead faith.*** We shall refer to them here as *active and passive faith.*

- When faith is *alive*—it is ***active*** and can be *seen or evidenced* in the life of the believer. *Active faith is faith with a witness.*

- When faith is *dead*—it is ***passive*** and *cannot be seen or evidenced* in the life of the believer. *Passive faith is faith without a witness.*

This is why James emphasizes works in relation to faith. James said that *just because one says that he has faith, his verbal declaration alone does not prove that he truly has faith.* He also says that *a declaration of* ***faith without works is dead, being***

alone. What does this mean?

- ***Passive faith***: is faith *without* proof. It is *dead* in that it produces or brings forth nothing.

- ***Active faith***: is faith *with proof.* It is *alive* in that it produces *fruit* (or faith-works) in the life of the believer.

Therefore, we might conclude that:

When faith is a living faith it is actively moving toward the promise or fulfillment of God's Word.

What Is Faith?

Now faith is the substance of things hoped for, the evidence of things not seen.

(Heb.11:1)

Let us take a closer look at *the dynamic nature of Abraham's faith.* The writer of Hebrews says that faith is both a *substance* and evidence. To Abraham, faith became:

- ***His substance*** (Gk. *hupostasis*) - assurance, confidence, firm trust, guarantee, or deed of title.

- ***His evidence*** (Gk. *elegchos*) - proof, or proof unto *conviction*, that what God "had promised, he was able also to perform" (Rom. 4:21).

Faith was to Abraham—*his firm trust, assurance, and guarantee of title (ownership) to the promises of God.* It was also his *proof unto conviction that God's Word would be fulfilled.*

Understanding Faith as Trust

To have faith is to have trust in and to act upon the Word of God.

In believing God, Abraham *trusted in* and *acted upon* the promises of God. *His trust in those promises resulted in his justification.* The apostle Paul characterizes Abraham's faith in the following manner:

And being not weak in faith, he considered not his own body now dead, when he was about an hundred years old, neither yet the deadness of Sarah's womb: He staggered not at the promise of God through unbelief; but was strong in faith, giving glory to God; And being fully persuaded that, what he had promised, he was able also to perform. And therefore it was imputed to him for righteousness.

(Rom.4: 19-22)

<u>*How Did Abraham Trust God?*</u>

- *He considered not his own body now dead (sterile) at 99 years old.*
- *He considered not the deadness (barrenness) of Sarah's womb.*
- *He staggered (wavered) not at the promise through unbelief.*
- *He gave glory to God in spite of the circumstances.*
- *He was fully persuaded that what God had promised, he was able to perform.*

The writer of Hebrews also reminds us:

But without faith it is impossible to please him: for he that cometh to God must believe that he is, and that he is a rewarder of them that diligently seek him.

(Heb.11:6)

Abraham had *faith in the promises* of God. He **saw** them afar off , was ***persuaded*** of them, and ***embraced them*** (Heb.11:13). And so:

<u>Living Faith Is</u>

- *Being able to* ***see God's promises fulfilled in the spirit realm.***
- *Being* ***persuaded or convinced beyond unbelief.***
- *Being able to* ***embrace God's Word no matter what*** *the circumstances suggest.*

Faith On Trial

That the trial of your faith, being much more precious than of gold that perisheth, though it be tried with fire, might be found unto praise and honour and glory at the appearing of Jesus Christ:
(1 Pet.1:7)

Faith is of no benefit whatsoever unless it is being tested or proven.

The offering of Isaac was *the ultimate test of Abraham's faith.* In a criminal court of law, the examiner of fact, usually a judge or jury, weighs the prosecution's evidence to determine if a defendant is guilty or not guilty of a crime with which he has been charged. Such evidence is considered as *proof of guilt.* This proof or evidence must be such that it meets a burden of proof standard. This burden of proof standard must be beyond a reasonable doubt. This process is called a *trial.*

During a spiritual trial, the believer's faith is put to the test, as was Abraham when he offered up Isaac.

<u>*The Antithesis of Faith is Unbelief*</u>

In the *spirit world,* like an advocate, *faith must present evidence or proof in the behalf of the believer.* This proof must be strong enough to overcome the objections raised by doubt and unbelief. Remember, the writer of Hebrews says *faith is the evi*dence (proof unto conviction) *of things not seen.* During a trial, faith must present evidence of a conviction of faith beyond the burden of doubt and unbelief raised by the accuser (Satan).

God's Word or promise is His testimony in behalf of the believer. The believer must trust in the testimony of God's Word regardless of what argument is put forth by circumstances, or the testimony and accusations of Satan, the accuser of the brethren (Job 1:7-11; Rev.12:10).

- *The believer's faith must be firm. He must have the* ***assurance*** *that he holds the* ***title*** *or* ***deed of ownership*** *to what God has* ***promised*** *him,* ***even when he does not see*** *with his natural eyes* ***any evidence*** *that the promise will be fulfilled.*

- *The believer must* ***trust God's Word*** *and must* ***ignore his senses, reasoning, the present circumstances*** *and* ***any argument of Satan*** *to the contrary.*

- *The believer must understand that his* ***faith alone*** *is his* ***guarantee*** *that God's Word or promise is His strong foundation and that He will bring it to pass.*

What Does Faith Do?

Through faith we understand that the worlds were framed by the word of God, so that things which are seen were not made of things which do appear.

(Heb.11:3)

It is important to understand—That *which God has promised us* ***already exists*** *in the spirit world.* It must however be appropriated or acquired. The universe exists because God's Word says it does. God *upholds all things by the Word of his power* (Heb.1:3). *God's Word therefore becomes the basis of all faith and any action done on his part* (Rom.10:17).

Faith is that which crosses over the dimensions of time and space and appropriates the promises of God.

That which God has promised the believer already exists in the dimensions of the spirit world. Faith brings these promises into our reality. In essence, faith "calleth those **things** which be not as though they were: (Rom. 4:17 emphasis added). *Faith embraces the eternity of NOW*. The writer of Hebrews speaks of faith as, "Now faith is.." (Heb. 11:1). So, why must faith be NOW faith?

We live in the dimensions of time and space. With God there is no reckoning of time or space. *God is a Spirit* (Jn. 4:24*). He transcends the dimensions of time and space and inhabits or dwells in eternity* (Isa. 57:15). *With God there is only one eternal NOW. Therefore, when God speaks in eternity, it is always NOW.*

Though man receives the promise (or the Word) in the space and point of reference called time, when God speaks, though in eternity, it is always and forever NOW. When we believe in God's Word or His promises, it must be NOW. Even though God may have spoken in our time yesterday, today, or 5,000 years ago. *To us, God's Word is a promise spoken in time but to God he still speaks in the eternal reality of NOW.*

What Is Saving Faith?

The scriptures teach that ***the faith that justifies is also the faith that saves.*** *Since salvation involves the process of justification, this is where many misunderstand and misapply James' teaching regarding faith and works.*

Because of James' emphasis on works, ***many have not understood what it means to be saved by faith and likewise have placed emphasis on obedience in order to be saved and eternally secure.*** *So, what then is saving faith?*

Saving faith is faith that is rooted and grounded in the finished work of Christ and appropriating the merit of His finished work for one's personal salvation.

Saving Faith Is

- ***Believing the gospel****—of the death, burial, and resurrection of Jesus Christ.*

- ***Trusting solely in the atonement****—of Christ's shed blood for salvation, the remission of sins and the believer's security* (1 Cor. 15: 1-5).

Saving faith is such that:

God only accepts the faith of the believer who trusts only in the finished work of the shed blood of Christ.

Those who perform good works by belief and trust in Buddha, Mohammed, themselves, or some other god or belief system may have faith evidenced by works. However, God does not recognize or accept their faith as the faith that saves or justifies. The grace believer understands that:

It is by enduring faith in the blood of Jesus alone that one is justified. Although works may follow one's faith, one is to put no faith (assurance, confidence, or trust) ***in one's works that he or she is righteous or justified before God.***

The ever present danger for the legalist is that he places his trust or faith in his own works that he will be justified (declared righteous) ***rather than in the finished work of Christ*** (Lk. 18:1).

The Principle of Dead Works

Therefore leaving the principles of the doctrine of Christ, let us go on unto perfection; not laying again the foundation of repentance from dead works, and of faith toward God,
(Heb. 6:1)

How much more shall the blood of Christ, who through the eternal Spirit offered himself without spot to God, purge your conscience from dead works to serve the living God?
(Heb. 9:14)

There is another very important principle that is often missed when considering faith and works. That is—*the principle of dead works*. The writer to the Hebrews *twice* mentions the *negative* nature of dead works. Just what are dead works?

Dead works are works that are wrought outside of faith in the blood of Jesus. *Dead works are not only* **works of unrighteousness,** *dead works are also* **works of self-righteousness.** Dead works are the works of the legalist. Why?

Legalism insists that saving faith involves having a combination of grace and law, or faith and works in order to be saved.

This is a subtle but dangerous mixture of **religion and humanism.** *This unholy union brought about through misplaced faith can be seen in various forms from Eden to Babylon.* Such is *the way of Cain* whom *Jude the Lord's brother, also warned about* (Jude11). Moreover, such were *the works of Cain* which we shall examine a little later (1 Jn. 3:12).

Suffice it to say, *if there is dead faith there are also dead works.* Yet, we are told time and again in scripture that our *"works of righteousness which we have done"* have *nothing whatsoever* to do with our eternal salvation (Eph. 2:8-9; Tit. 3:5).

In Hebrews 6:1, notice *the association of dead works contrasted with faith toward God.* Why does the writer of Hebrews point us *away* from dead works and to *faith toward God*? Yea, we are even told to *repent* from dead works. Why? Because, *man cannot be justified or saved through dead works. The believer's faith must forever be toward God and away from himself.*

- ***Dead works represent the self-righteous efforts of man to attain righteousness and right standing with God without placing absolute faith in the blood of Jesus.***

- ***Dead works of self-righteousness are in themselves evil, remove us from the atonement, and separate us from faith toward God.*** (Gen. 4:5; 1 Jn. 3:12).

Works—The Fruit of Faith

Let your light so shine before men, that they may see your good works, and glorify your Father which is in heaven.

(Matt. 5:16)

And let ours also learn to maintain good works for necessary uses, that they be not unfruitful.

(Tit. 3:14)

Let us now examine the scriptural relationship of *works as the fruit of faith*. Because of his emphasis on works, it would casually appear that James spoke as a legalist. However,

James endeavored to teach us

- *Faith is* ***wrought with*** *and* ***not apart from*** *works.*
- *Faith is* ***dead*** *if it presents no* ***evidence*** *that it exists.*

Two Kinds of Works

It is very important to understand and distinguish that **good works by themselves do not always represent living faith.** We are primarily concerned with distinguishing between *two kinds of works* here.

Dead works and Faith-works

1) **Dead works**: *Acts or deeds of* ***man's righteousness*** *that are* ***wrought apart from*** *faith in* ***the finished work of Christ*** *at Calvary.* ***Dead works spring forth from a spirit of self-righteousness and are motivated by pride. Dead works have*** *a form of godliness* ***(as religious humanism)*** *but deny the power thereof* (2 Tim. 3:5).

2) **Faith-works**: ***Acts or deeds of the believer in the finished work of Christ*** *at Calvary. Faith - works spring forth from the Spirit of grace and* ***are motivated by love and humility.*** *Faith-works* ***are***

wrought in God *and* ***have the promises or Word of God at their core*** (Jn. 3:21).

The works that James is speaking about are not the dead works of self-righteousness. The works that James is speaking about are the ***evidence of the believer's faith in God's Word or promises. Faith-works are rooted, grounded and established in:***

- *The righteousness of God*
- *The finished work of Calvary*
- *The principles of substitution and atonement*

The truth is—*When faith is alive, it brings forth fruit. Faith-works are the* ***fruit*** *of living faith that* ***prove*** *that* ***faith is alive!*** Because of the negative aspect of dead works and the positive aspect of faith-works,

The writers of the New Testament often referred to the works of faith as fruit.

Even James speaks of *the fruit of righteousness* (Jam. 3:18). So, how do we define fruit?

Fruit is the supernatural outgrowth, byproduct, or result of faith.

In understanding works as fruit, it helps to visualize faith as ***a seed*** *that when planted and cultivated, matures to produce the fruit of righteousness.*

John the Baptist spoke of works as fruit when he said, " bring forth therefore fruits meet for repentance" (Matt. 3:8). He was referring to *the good works* that would be *the result* of genuine repentance. As we consider works as *the fruit of faith,* we are reminded *that,*

The fruit of righteousness is possible only because of our spiritual union and vital relationship with Christ.

This relationship is vividly portrayed in the metaphor of *the vine and the branches* of John chapter 15 and demonstrates that:

It is indeed Christ who is doing the works and producing the fruit in the believer through the indwelling Holy Spirit. The illustration of the vine and branches underscores the necessity of the believer abiding in Christ and He in the believer; without which, no fruit is possible.

For Christ said of this vital relationship, "…for without me ye can do nothing" (Jn. 15:5). It is because of this vital and fruitful relationship of the believer with Christ that Paul could say:

For if Abraham were justified by works, he hath whereof to glory; but not before God (Rom. 4:2). Why? Because Paul understood:

For it is God which worketh in you both to will and to do of his good pleasure (Phil. 2:13; Gal. 2:20.) In other words:

Christ is performing all the good works in and through us, and He deserves all of the glory for any fruit manifested in the life of the believer.

Wherever fruit is manifest in the life of the believer, whether as *souls won* to God (Prov. 11:30), the *fruit of the Spirit* (Gal. 5:22, Eph. 5:9), or as *good works* defined as faith-works (Matt. 5:16), it must be understood that:

All fruit in the life of the believer is the supernatural outgrowth or by-product of the vital and spiritual union of Christ working in the life of the believer. The believer cannot bring forth any fruit of himself that is pleasing or acceptable to God (Rom. 8:8).

Jesus said, "That which is born of the flesh is flesh; and that which is born of the Spirit is spirit" (Jn. 3:6).

10

<u>*The Two Coverings*</u>

And the eyes of them both were opened, and they knew that they were naked; and they sewed fig leaves together, and made themselves aprons.

Unto Adam also and to his wife did the LORD God make coats of skins, and clothed them.

(Gen. 3:7, 21)

Adam & Eve

In order to fully understand the controversy between the doctrine of grace and the doctrine of works, we must start from the very dawn of man's history. For *it was in the Garden of Eden that man first received his experience with the principles of law and grace. Since Genesis is the seedbed for the doctrine of salvation,* we should examine *how grace, law* and *legalism* presented itself there.

***It is impossible to understand New Testament salvation by grace without first having a basic understanding of the redemptive theology revealed in the book of Genesis*.**

The events surrounding *the Fall* and the early history of man reveal that the *enmity and struggle between law and grace* is as old as *Adam and Eve* and can even be seen in their children, *Cain and Abel.* An amazing and consistent principle throughout scripture is that:

The righteousness of God is revealed from *faith to faith* ***and not from faith to works*** (Heb. 6:1; Rom. 1:17).

Yet, consistently *throughout* scripture man has sought just the opposite. *He often forsakes faith in the blood and seeks to be justified by his works.* The result is *legalism.* In the following examples of *misplaced fa*ith we shall see that:

The legalist always departs from (the principle of justification by) ***faith to embrace*** (the principle of justification by) ***works.*** ***Yet, God always leads man to the place of repentance from dead works and to faith toward God*** (Heb. 6:1).

The Edenic Covenant

If we are to be true to the scriptures, we must acknowledge that:

Adam was the first man to institute a system of legalism or righteousness through works.

Adam's man-made covering for sin was no less an act of self-righteousness than any other religious covering fashioned by man today. However, Adam's remedy for his sinful act was *rejected* outright by God! What does this mean to us today? First, let's put some things into perspective. Before Adam fell, he was absolutely righteous, one with God and kept the demands *of the law of the garden.* This is often referred to as *The Edenic Covenant.* God gave this to Adam.

And the LORD God commanded the man, saying, Of every tree of the garden thou mayest freely eat:
But of the tree of the knowledge of good and evil, thou shalt not eat of it: for in the day that thou eatest thereof thou shalt surely die.
(Gen. 2:16-17)

The Curse of the Law

However, the moment Adam sinned his *fellowship with God*

was broken. Adam became *a transgressor* and *a debtor* to the law God had given him. Because he was now a *sinner*, he was *no longer able to keep the demands of the law and came under its curse.* Remember:

The curse of the law is not only death but also the inability of man to fulfill the demands of the law (Gal. 3:10). Two things I want to stress here are:

1) ***The law always begins with a demand*** (Gen. 2:16-17). *In essence,* ***the law is little more than a legal demand for righteousness.*** *More importantly,* ***the law provides no remedy*** *for the transgressor;* ***it promises only condemnation and death.***

2) ***Grace always begins with a promise*** (Gen. 3:15). *Grace* ***promises and provides a remedy*** *for the transgressor. Grace* ***provides righteousness as a gift*** *to all those who will receive it by faith, without the deeds of the law!*

Grace In the Garden

Adam was the first legalist converted from works to faith.

When Adam and Eve sinned, their *eyes were opened* and man's *conscience* was awakened. *For the first time in history man experienced guilt, shame, condemnation, and fear.* These were the immediate spiritual consequences of transgressing *the law of the garden.*

Adam's first response to sin was to hide himself from God. Since ***the law of the garden*** *provided no remedy for sin*, Adam fashioned *a covering* with his own hands. *He chose* fig leaves. Adam did not realize that God was already one giant step ahead of him. He had no way of knowing about God's divine drama to which he was now committed. *Adam was about to receive his first lesson in grace theology.*

When we say we can find ***grace in the garden,*** we mean exactly that. *In the Garden of Eden, we have the bedrock upon which New Testament salvation is firmly secured.* We understand this because:

Grace is predicated on the principles of substitution and atonement.

After acknowledging and openly confessing his sin before God, Adam's *self-made* covering was rejected. Why was it rejected? *It was rejected because it was fashioned contrary to the principles of substitution and atonement.* It was the result of *Adam's own works.* Likewise, the legalist must come to the understanding that:

God will never accept a covering for sin that does not fully embody the finished work of Jesus Christ at Calvary.

Does the covering God gave to Adam and to his wife reflect the *redemptive theology of grace* and *the principles of substitution and atonement?* Let's take a closer look at the two coverings.

ADAM'S COVERING	***GOD'S COVERING***
1) Fig leaves	***Coats of skins***
2) The works of Adam	***The works of God***
3) Rejected by God	***Accepted by God***
4) Adam took part in	***Adam took no part in***
5) Substitution absentS	***ubstitution present***
6) Atonement absent	***Atonement present***
7) Faith in works	***Faith in the blood***

- *While Adam's covering was of fig leaves,* ***the work of his own hands****, God's covering of skins was* ***the work of God alone.***
- *Adam's* ***covering of works was rejected*** *by God, while God's*

covering of skins was accepted.

- *Adam* ***took part in providing his covering*** *of fig leaves, but* ***Adam did nothing to secure or make sure for himself the covering of skins.***

- *Adam had* ***no part whatsoever in the sacrifice of atonement*** *made by God Himself.* ***Adam's works were not part of the process and were not taken into account.*** *It was* ***all the work of God Himself.***

- *Adam's covering* ***in no way demonstrated and provided for the principles of substitution and atonement.***

- *God's* ***covering provided for and demonstrated the principles of substitution and atonement.***

- *Adam's covering* ***demonstrated that he had faith only in his works.***

- *God's covering* ***demonstrated Adam's faith was only in the blood.***

You see, ***Adam had faith and works.*** However, at first *his faith was misplaced.* Adam *repented of his dead works of self-righteousness*, removed his fig leaves, and by receiving the coat of skins, he openly expressed his newly found *faith in the blood atonement.*

Faith in Works or Faith in the Blood?

Like Adam, the legalist insists that he must participate to some degree in his salvation and that his righteous works must also be taken into account before he can be eternally saved and justified before God.

It is here that *the legalist must be careful and repent,* for he is standing on *unholy* ground. He is not alone, however; *the Mormons and the Jehovah Witnesses believe likewise.*

Do not be fooled by the mere presence of faith and works in a person's life.

It is not enough to ask if the believer is justified by faith or by works. Neither is it enough to recognize the existence of both faith and works in the life of the believer.

We must delve deeper to resolve the question:

In what or in whom does that faith reside?

Where is the believer's faith supposed to be rooted and grounded; in their works of righteousness or ***in the blood of the lamb*** (Tit. 3:5; Rev. 12:11)?

The first promise of redemption through grace is given in the book of Genesis. Theologians refer to it as the *proto-evangelicum* or *first good news.* It declares:

And I will put enmity between thee and the woman, and between thy seed and her seed; it shall bruise thy head, and thou shalt bruise his heel.

(Gen. 3:15)

The *Jehovah's Witnesses* believe that God clothed Adam and Eve with the decaying skin of animals that died of natural causes. Furthermore, they believe that Adam and Eve died in their sin and were lost. How absurd!

It is no mystery that God clothed Adam and Eve with *coats of skins* and these were the skins of a spotless innocent *lamb.* No doubt, *the stain of blood* was fresh upon them when God presented them *a covering* for their *nakedness, shame,* and *guilt,* which they bore.

Behold the Lamb of God!

We know that *in the mind of God, the sacrifice of Christ was predetermined before Adam had fallen* (Acts 2:23). *The plan of redemption was no secret to Him. It was not an afterthought. It was forethought.*

John the revelator writes that Christ is "... the Lamb slain from the foundation of the world" (Rev. 13:8).

Peter declares of Christ, "Who verily was foreordained before the foundation of the world, but was manifest in these last times for you," (1 Pet. 1:20).

John the Baptist also proclaimed, *"Behold the Lamb of God, which taketh away the sin of the world"* (Jn. 1:29).

In summary: *It was no less an act of divine grace in the garden when God shed the blood of the innocent to atone for the sin of the guilty.* Though it cost the life of an innocent, it was *his free gift to Adam and Eve* (See Rom. 5:15-18). Contrary to what the Jehovah Witnesses believe, ***Adam and Eve were not lost.***

God had Himself done all the works necessary to provide man with this atonement. It cost man nothing. They did not have to work for it, earn it, or maintain it. They had only to believe and receive the covering that God provided for them.

This proves once again that:

God's principle of substitution and atonement operates through the principle of grace and it is consistent throughout scripture.

If we have learned anything from the lesson of Adam and Eve, *we will be careful to shun any form of legalism's doctrine of salvation through works.* Adam (as have many since) *may have started down the road of legalism and self-righteousness through works,* but he turned around and became a grace believer. Grace is *the free gift* of God's unmerited favor.

11

The Two Offerings

And in process of time it came to pass, that Cain brought of the fruit of the ground an offering unto the LORD.

And Abel, he also brought of the firstlings of his flock and of the fat thereof.

And the LORD had respect unto Abel and to his offering:

But unto Cain and to his offering he had not respect. And Cain was very wroth, and his countenance fell.

(Gen. 4:3-4)

The Misappropriation of Faith

Although much has already been shared about *grace theology* and *legalism,* we have barely scratched the surface. Other aspects of grace and legalism have yet to be examined. At the risk of being redundant, I would like to share some other important aspects of *grace theology* and the dangers of legalism. Among these is *the misappropriation of faith.*

The misappropriation of faith is at the heart of legalism.

When I say that *faith can be misappropriated*, I mean that *faith can be misplaced or placed in someone or something other than what it was originally intended.*

Cain Falls From Grace

Perhaps the best concise Old Testament example of this is also found in the book of Genesis. Soon after the lesson of *grace in the Garden,* we arrive at an altar where two sons have each brought an offering to the LORD. The two sons are Cain and Abel. Let 's look at this man, Cain.

Cain was the first man to fall from grace and institute a system of legalism.

What do we mean by *falling from grace?* Isn't this expression often used to characterize someone who has committed some reprehensible sin? How often have we heard about *"so and so"* and his or her *fall from grace*? Like the phrase "*yoke of bondage,*" we explained earlier on,

The expression "fallen from grace" is also improperly used by many both in and outside of the church.

Usually, when we hear the phrase *fallen from grace,* we associate it with some *moral failure on the part of someone who has committed sin.* However, what people really mean is that *"so and so" fell into sin.*

It is my opinion that it is entirely *improper and unscriptural* for believers to use the expression *fallen from grace* in this manner. What did the Apostle Paul have in mind when he used the expression *"fallen from grace"?*

Christ is become of no effect unto you, whosoever of you are justified by the law; ye are ***fallen from grace.***

(Gal. 5:4 emphasis added)

Did Paul use this phrase to describe someone falling into sin? By studying the context and Paul's use of this phrase, the answer is no! *Fallen from grace does not mean fallen into sin.*

Fallen from grace means falling or departing from the doctrine or principle of salvation through grace alone, and

embracing another gospel.

It must be understood that:

One does not and cannot fall from grace because of moral failure or an act or lifestyle of sin. Falling from grace has nothing whatsoever to do with sin.

Falling from grace has to do with departing from the truth and embracing another gospel. In this instance, it had to do with legalism—the principle of righteousness through works (Gal. 6:1-9).

Cain did not fall from grace because of an act of sin. Cain fell from grace because of his misplaced faith. Allow me to explain.

Cain's error was much deeper and far more serious than a mere act of sin, such as adultery or murder. In fact, *Cain actually fell from grace some time before he murdered his brother Abel.* We know that ***God had already rejected him and his religion of works prior to his sin of murder***. So, what then do we mean when we say *Cain fell from grace*?

When we say Cain fell from grace, we are saying that Cain fell, or departed from, the doctrine or principles of substitution and atonement as revealed in the Garden of Eden, and embraced the legalism of self-righteousness and justification through works.

This is what the Bible and the apostle Paul have in mind when they speak of *falling from grace*. Yet, today it seems that much of the church world has given a new meaning to this verse.

From Legalism to Apostasy

You see, *Adam did not fall from grace*. Adam fell from *a state of innocence;* he had *a brief encounter with legalism*, repented, and entered *a state of grace*. What do we mean by a state of grace?

A state of grace is a position or standing of redemptive favor

and blessing based on faith in the blood atonement.

God atoned for Adam's sin through the sacrifice of a *lamb* in the garden. *Before the Fall, Adam had no prior knowledge of substitution and atonement.* However, *Cain did have this knowledge* at the time of his offering in Genesis chapter 4. Therefore, I believe that Cain's error was much more serious than that of Adam. What was Cain's error?

Cain departed from the faith.

This *faith* or *belief system* was previously delivered to him by his father, Adam. If this is true, then *Cain was himself a legalist.* Not only was Cain a legalist:

Cain was the first true apostate mentioned in scripture.

What is an apostate?

An apostate is one who falls away or departs from the belief system of substitution and atonement commonly called "the faith" (Jude 3).

Some might ask, "Why should we consider Cain an apostate in the first place? The answer is simple. The epistle of Jude says he is (Jude 1,11). Cain was the second man after the fall to establish ***a belief system of righteousness through works.*** Like his father,

Cain instituted a religious system of righteousness based on faith and works.

However, *it* ***was based on faith in his works*** *rather than faith in the blood atonement* (a blood sacrifice).

In embracing a system of righteousness through works, Cain was misappropriating faith that was given to him by God. This faith was to be placed only in the true sacrifice of atonement (Rom. 3:25).

Faith is a gift from God (Eph. 2:8-9). The scriptures declare that God "hath dealt to every man the measure of faith" (Rom. 12:3). However,

It is man who determines where the gift of faith will be placed or reside. Man can either place that faith (trust) in the finished work of Christ, or in something or someone else, including his own works of righteousness.

In Christ, we understand that *the righteousness of God is revealed* ***from faith to faith*** (Rom.1:17). The writer of Hebrews tells us that:

By faith Abel offered unto God a *more excellent sacrifice than Cain.*
(Heb.11:4)

Abel did not offer his sacrifice according to fancy; *he offered his sacrifice according to faith.* The scriptures declare:

So then faith cometh by hearing, and hearing by the word of God.
(Rom.10:17)

From whom did Cain and Abel hear the Word of God? No doubt from Adam, and perhaps from God Himself. We know that *God spoke to Cain personally* (Gen. 4:9). ***Cain and Abel both knew what God required—an offering according to faith!*** They knew they could not please God ***without faith*** and were no doubt instructed in how to please God (Heb. 11:6).

Yet, why didn't God accept Cain and his offering? A lot of speculation abounds as to why God did not receive the offering of Cain. However, *it was not just Cain's offering that was rejected; Cain was rejected himself.* This brings out another important truth:

If God does not accept an individual on the basis of the shed blood of Jesus Christ, He does not accept their self-righteous works.

What was wrong with Cain that God did not accept him and his offering? Although there are different kinds of offerings in scripture, *meal, grain, drink, etc., it* ***is believed by many that because Cain offered a sacrifice without blood*** *(the fruit of the ground),* ***God rejected him on that basis.*** While this does have merit, I believe the answer lies in the possibility that:

Cain offered his offering in pride and self-righteousness.

Cain, like his father and brother, was *religious, had faith, and was a worshiper of God.* However:

Beneath Cain's religion, faith, and worship was the unrepented sin of self-righteousness and spiritual pride. Self-righteousness and spiritual pride are among the telltale signs of legalism. Cain trusted in his own works that he was righteous, and by them he expected to receive the favor and acceptance of God.

To demonstrate this, ***Cain commended his own works to God by bringing an offering of the fruit of the ground*** (Gen. 4:3). By approaching God in this ***manner, he wanted God to accept him on the basis of his own works.*** Naturally, *God rejected him and Cain got angry.* Ultimately, he slew his own brother and ended up a vagabond and *perhaps the first reprobate* in scripture (1 Jn. 3:12).

Cain repeated the error of his father, but he did not follow his father's repentance and faith toward God (Heb. 6:1).

Had Cain done *well,* he would no doubt have been accepted (Gen. 4:6). *Not on the basis of his works of righteousness, but on the same basis as Abel—a blood sacrifice of substitution and atonement* (Heb. 11:4).

Abel's offering typified faith in the finished work of Christ.

However, Cain chose rather to "abide.. still in unbelief" (Rom. 11:23) and therefore hardening his heart, *he found no place of repentance* (Heb. 12:17).

What was it that led Cain into legalism?

Pride** and **self-righteousness** led Cain into legalism. **Legalism led Cain into apostasy**.* Cain *fell away* from *the truth of* ***righteousness through faith in the blood atonement and *sought to be justified by his own works.*

Why Is Legalism So Dangerous?

Legalism is dangerous business. Why is legalism so dangerous? In my opinion, *legalism is so dangerous because it is so subtle:*

- *Legalism is another form of **religious humanism.***
- *Legalism **undermines** and **challenges justification by faith** in the blood alone.*
- *Legalism **teaches that faith is equal to obedience** and that **obedience results in righteousness** with God.*
- *Legalism **makes man responsible for his own salvation** rather than the grace, power, and promises of God.*

Many believers, including preachers, do not understand the theology of faith and works. The misappropriation of faith causes serious problems for the legalist, because legalism requires man to place faith in his works in order to be saved.

Most religions of the world, including ***the religion of humanism*** *require man to look to man or within man for the answers to salvation.* However, *God requires that we look to Him for the answers to salvation* (Isa. 45:22).

The legalist sincerely believes he is saved by faith; however, his faith is not rooted and grounded only in the blood of Jesus Christ and His finished work. The legalist's faith appears to be

rooted in Christ, yet it is actually grounded in the legalist's own works (Jn. 19:30).

In essence, *a legalist's salvation depends on God's acceptance of his works.* How sad when:

The legalist insists on trusting in his own works of righteousness in order to be saved, rather than in the righteousness of Jesus Christ. That is why the legalist is never completely sure of his salvation and frets over losing it, because he is never completely sure his lifetime of works will pass the test and be accepted of God, just like Cain.

On what basis does God accept any man? God will only accept us as we are accepted in His *beloved, as* we are in His Son, Jesus Christ.

- *In Christ, we are righteous.*
- *In Christ, we are holy.*
- *In Christ, we are perfect in God's sight.*

Without Christ we can be none of the above. If we stand alone in our own works of righteousness, we are all "as an unclean thing, and all our righteousnesses are as filthy rags;" (Isa. 64:6).

12

The Two Prayers

And he spake this parable unto certain which trusted in themselves that they were righteous, and despised others: Two men went up into the temple to pray; the one a Pharisee, and the other a publican.

The Pharisee stood and prayed thus with himself, God, I thank thee, that I am not as other men are, extortioners, unjust, adulterers, or even as this publican.

I fast twice in the week, I give tithes of all that I possess.

And the publican, standing afar off, would not lift up so much as his eyes unto heaven, but smote upon his breast, saying, God be merciful to me a sinner.

I tell you, this man went down to his house justified rather than the other: for every one that exalteth himself shall be abased; and he that humbleth himself shall be exalted.

(Lk. 18:9-14)

I want to give you a New Testament example of misplaced faith. For this we turn to the gospel of Luke and to Christ's parable of:

The Pharisee and The Publican

Even our prayers can reveal the extent to which we have embraced and held on to legalism.

In this parable, our Lord uses the prayers of two men to teach us something about the *theology of grace* and the dangers of legalism. Since prayer is an act of devotion toward God,

We must take care to keep our prayer life free of legalistic prayer patterns.

I believe we can tell much about our personal theology and our own understanding of grace by listening to and examining our own prayers.

Since I have embraced grace theology, *I frequently find myself praying legalistic prayers.* I recognize them instantly. Rather than thanking God for the things He has already bestowed upon me through grace, such as His favor, blessings, etc., I find myself pleading for them as if I am trying to be worthy or deserving of them somehow.

Three Things That Identify A Legalist

In the parable of the Pharisee and the Publican, we are given insight into the root causes of legalism. Looking at the parable there are at least three things that identify a legalist. They are *spiritual pride, self-righteousness, and judgmentalism.*

- *A religious spirit of* ***self-exaltation*** *through boasting and spiritual pride.*

- *A religious spirit of* ***self-righteousness*** *through justification by works.*

- *A religious spirit of* ***judgmentalism*** *through condemnation of others.*

At the very root of legalism is *the spirit of self-exaltation, or* ***the sin of spiritual pride****. Pride (self-exaltation) is the oldest form of sin in the universe.*

The Danger of Spiritual Pride

Spiritual pride is manifested as ***a religious spirit*** *of self-righteousness and self-exaltation while despising or condemning others. Why is spiritual pride so dangerous in the life of a believer?*

Spiritual pride is so dangerous because it is so ***subtle and deceptive,*** *especially when it is cloaked and shrouded in the robes of religion.* **Pride is the mother of all sin.** It is a hidden or secret sin. It is ***an iniquity of the heart and of the spirit*** *that left unchecked will eventually manifest itself in the form of legalism* (Psa. 90:8). Isn't it interesting that,

This parable teaches us that self-exaltation, self-righteousness and self-adulation are all related to one another (Lk. 18:14)? I ask you to remember—***what was Lucifer's sin?*** Was not Lucifer's sin ***the sin of PRIDE?*** Was not this *iniquity found* **within** him (Ezek. 28:15)? Pride is a very deceptive sin because, as in Lucifer's case, ***it blinds us to our own corruption*** (Ezek. 28:17).

Jesus sees spiritual pride or self-exaltation as the root of all self-righteousness.

Self-righteousness leads to self-adulation (self-praise or boasting). It is the *delusion and infatuation with one's own works* that allows the legalist to be *critical of others and to hold others and their works in contempt.* Yet, God reveals many times in His Word that:

God chose salvation by way of the cross so that man could not glory or boast in achieving salvation by any other means (Eph. 2:9).

That's why the Apostle Paul said to the Galatians, "But **God forbid** that I should **glory**, save in **the cross** of our Lord Jesus Christ," (Gal. 6:14). Paul further said to the Ephesians that they were saved, **"...Not of works, lest any man should boast"** (Eph. 2:9). Paul teaches us that:

As believers, we are only to boast in the finished work Christ accomplished in our behalf at Calvary.

It is therefore clear to the *grace believer,* that in providing salvation through the cross,

God took special care to warn and protect man from the snare of the sin of pride, knowing that this is how Lucifer corrupted himself and fell from his first estate.

Paul therefore admonished Timothy that a bishop must not be "a novice, lest **being lifted up with pride** he fall into the condemnation of the devil" (1 Tim. 3:6 emphasis added). In my opinion:

Salvation through works is the biggest deception of the devil and of the age. Righteousness through works (legalism) ***is the devil's biggest lie, and many believe it lock, stock, and barrel! Legalism is so deceptive that those drawn within its grasp can hardly escape without the help of God.***

The Legalist's Prayer

We find each of the identifying characteristics of a legalist in the Pharisee's prayer: *spiritual pride, judgmentalism, and self-righteousness*. The first clue that the Pharisee was also a legalist *was the Pharisee's exalted state of pride*. Rather than approach God in *a spirit of humility*, the Pharisee **"stood and prayed thus with himself"** (vs. 11, emphasis added).

Next, we hear him expressing ***self-praise and judgmentalism*** by saying, "I thank thee, that **I am not as other men are**, extortioners, unjust, adulterers, or even as this publican" (vs. 11, emphasis added).

Finally, he concludes by boasting of his righteous works by declaring, "I fast twice in the week, I give tithes of all that I possess" (vs. 12. What is more troubling is:

The Pharisee is unaware of the deception that is taking place within his own heart and life.

<u>Like the Pharisee in our parable.</u>

- *The legalist believes that he will be justified (declared righteous) and* ***find favor*** *with God* ***because of*** *his piety and devotion.*

- *The legalist believes (due to his misplaced faith), he will be justified because of* ***his works****, and therefore* ***focuses on his own works of righteousness*** *rather than on the grace and mercy of God.*

- *The legalist can* ***often be found comparing his works*** *with the faults and shortcomings of those around him.*

However, the legalist derives *a false sense of comfort and security* from comparing himself to other believers (2 Cor. 10:12). *It is a false sense of security because he does not yet understand how he can be truly justified.*

And so, legalists find themselves, "**ignorant of God's righteousness**, and **going about to establish their own righteousness, have not submitted themselves unto the righteousness of God"** (Rom. 10:3).

The Grace Believer's Prayer

In contrast to the Pharisee, *the publican's prayer was void of pride, judgmentalism and self-righteousness.* Jesus said, 'This man went down to his house **justified** rather than the other:" (Luke 18:14, emphasis added). Why?

The publican approached God in a spirit of humility with an *abiding sense of God's holiness and his own sinfulness.*

How do we know this? The scripture says *he* was "standing afar off, and would not lift up so much as his eyes unto heaven." He was full of *contrition* and *brokenness*, for he smote upon his breast, *owning his own sinful nature*, saying, "God, be merciful to me a sinner." In summary—like the publican:

- *The grace believer* ***only sees himself in the light of God's grace and mercy,*** *without which he knows he could never be justified.*

- *The grace believer* ***confesses his inability to keep the righteous demands of the law*** *and* ***always approaches God remembering*** *that* ***he is himself a sinner.***

- *The grace believer* ***has faith only in the mercy of God, the blood of Jesus Christ, and God's ability to save him.***

In light of this, allow me ask, would *you rather be the Pharisee or the publican?*

The Workers of Iniquity

Not every one that saith unto me, Lord, Lord, shall enter into the kingdom of heaven; but he that doeth the will of my Father which is in heaven.

Many will say to me in that day, Lord, Lord, have we not prophesied in thy name? and in thy name have cast out devils? and in thy name done many wonderful works?

And then will I profess unto them, I never knew you: depart from me, ye that work iniquity.

(Matt. 7:21-23)

To a legalist, it is quite natural and appropriate for a man to commend himself and his works to God. Another example of this is found in the seventh chapter of Matthew.

Here, we are brought to a *judgment* where Christ presides. It is unclear which judgment is represented here, since there is more than one judgment in scripture. Is it the *Judgment (bema) Seat of Christ* (Rom. 14:10), the *Judgment of the Nations* at the return of Christ inaugurating the *millennial kingdom* (Matt. 25: 31-34), or the *White Throne Judgment* after the millennium?

Personally, I *believe this judgment is not the Judgment (bema) Seat of Christ or the White Throne Judgment.* Why? Those who are present at the *Bema seat* judgment have *already been translated at the rapture* (his appearing) *and will inherit the millennial kingdom* (2 Tim. 4:1). They are judged *prior* to Christ's literal return to earth and are present at the marriage supper of the Lamb (Rom. 14:10).

Furthermore, this judgment cannot be the *White Throne Judg*ment because *the White Throne Judgment takes place after the millennial kingdom and is the final judgment for man.* This judgment does not occur on Earth and is reserved for unbelievers and possibly millennial kingdom believers (Matt. 13:41; Rev. 20:11-15). *I believe the judgment referred to here corresponds to or runs concurrent with the Judgment of the Nations.*

The apostle Paul reveals that two judgments of *the quick and the dead* are yet to take place (2 Tim. 4:1; Matt. 25: 31-46). They are to take place at *His appearing* (the rapture), and seven (7) years later at *His kingdom* (the revelation).

- ***The Judgment (bema) Seat of Christ*** *occurs after the rapture of the church,* **at his appearing** (Rom. 14:10). *This judgment is only for believers.*

- ***The Judgment of the Nations*** *occurs after Christ's Second Coming,* **at his kingdom** (Matt. 25:32).

Related passages would suggest these *workers of iniquity* are either *Jewish converts who either heard or preached the gospel of the kingdom* in the same manner as the *twelve apostles* and the *seventy* (70) *witnesses* during Christ's First Advent, or *representative of the Jewish nation as a whole at his Second Advent* (Lk. 10:1,17; Matt. 24:14).

It is also possible that in this group are also *tribulation saints* who are Christ's witnesses during *the time of Jacob's trouble* (Jer. 30:7), as there will be no church present on earth during their ministry. However, as the *seventy* (70) and as the *two witnesses* in the book of the Revelation, they are empowered to perform miracles in Christ's name (Lk. 13:24-30; Rev. 11:3-11).

Whoever they are and whatever judgment is referred to here, *these workers of iniquity were denied entrance to the millennial kingdom.* Why? Some suggest that they were denied entrance because they were disobedient to the Word or otherwise unrighteous. This is

an assumption based on Christ's teaching of *the two foundations* (Matt. 7:24-47). They *heard the sayings of Christ and did them not.* The text does not say they were disobedient or unrighteousness (no doubt they were). However, the text does say they *were workers of iniquity*. I ask you to consider another possibility.
Could the iniquity in this instance be the same iniquity found in Lucifer in the form of self-righteousness, pride, and boasting (Ezk. 28:14-17)? I believe it is. If you will note carefully, in defense of their rejection it is plain to see, *their only argument was to boast of the wonderful works they had done in Christ's name.* Isn't it also interesting that:

At no time did they ever mention having been forgiven their sins in the name of Jesus? Neither did they plead the blood of Jesus ***alone*** *as the* ***basis*** *for their* ***right*** *to enter the kingdom of heaven.*

Why didn't they mention the blood? *Could it be because they thought they could enter the kingdom on the basis of their "many wonderful works?" No wonder Christ disowned them and denied knowing them as their personal Savior.*

It is my view that ***they were denied entrance to the kingdom because they did what so many others before them had done. Like the Pharisee, they trusted in themselves that they were righteous, rather than in Christ*** (Lk. 18: 9). ***I believe they were legalists.***

When one departs from the principles of grace (substitution and atonement), he will inevitably be lured into the bramble of legalism and find himself in the snare of righteousness through works.

This account of the workers of iniquity teaches us that regardless of your works,

Those who trust in their works that they will be saved are going to be sadly disappointed in the Day of Judgment. In the Day of Judgment, many will find out, oh, but too late, that their faith was indeed misplaced.

<u>*Three important things to remember*</u>

1) *Where there is* ***no faith in the blood,*** *there can be* ***no atonement.***

2) *Where there is* ***no atonement,*** *there is* ***no forgiveness*** *for sin.*

3) *Where there is* ***no forgiveness of sin,*** *there can be* ***no salvation.***

In summary, like the Pharisee and others we have studied, ***the workers of iniquity went from faith to works rather than from faith to faith*** (Rom. 1:17). This further reveals that until the *perfect age* there will be legalists in all dispensations.

One does not have to live under the Old Testament of the law to be a legalist. One can live under any dispensation and be a legalist. One is a legalist simply because he embraces the concept of righteousness through human merit **(works).**

PART III

ELECTION

&

THE CALLING OF THE BELIEVER

Election:

That act of God,
whereby
He through sovereign grace,
and
according to his eternal purpose,
elects or chooses the believer in Christ,
and predestines him
to the effectual calling
and adoption of sonship,
without
any regard for
works or merit
on the part
of the one elected.

*According as **he hath chosen us** in him before the foundation of the world, that we should be holy and without blame before him in love:*

Having predestinated us unto the adoption of children by Jesus Christ to himself, according to the good pleasure of his will,

To the praise of the glory of his grace, wherein he hath made us accepted in the beloved.

In whom we have redemption through his blood, the forgiveness of sins, according to the riches of his grace;

Wherein he hath abounded toward us in all wisdom and prudence;

Having made known unto us the mystery of his will, according to his good pleasure which he hath purposed in himself:

That in the dispensation of the fulness of times he might gather together in one all things in Christ, both which are in heaven, and which are on earth; even in him:

In whom also we have obtained an inheritance, being predestinated according to the purpose of him who worketh all things after the counsel of his own will:

That we should be to the praise of his glory, who first trusted in Christ.

In whom ye also trusted, after that ye heard the word of truth, the gospel of your salvation: in whom also after that ye believed, ye were sealed with that holy Spirit of promise,

Which is the earnest of our inheritance until the redemption of the purchased possession, unto the praise of his glory.

Eph. 1:4-14

13

The Two Sons

For this is the word of promise, At this time will I come, and Sarah shall have a son.

And not only this; but when Rebecca also had conceived by one, even by our father Isaac;

(For the children being not yet born, neither having done any good or evil, that the purpose of God according to election might stand, not of works, but of him that calleth;)

It was said unto her, The elder shall serve the younger. As it is written, Jacob have I loved, but Esau have I hated.

What shall we say then? Is there unrighteousness with God? God forbid.

For he saith to Moses, I will have mercy on whom I will have mercy, and I will have compassion on whom I will have compassion.

So then it is not of him that willeth, nor of him that runneth, but of God that sheweth mercy.

(Rom. 9:9-16)

It Began With A Promise

In these verses *the Apostle Paul gives the most powerful and persuasive argument for salvation through grace that I can find anywhere in the scriptures*. He begins with *a promise made to Abraham* (Rom. 9:9), and unfolds *the mystery* of *predestination* and *election* through Isaac (Rom. 9:10-11) and Jacob (Rom. 9:12), linking these doctrines to the *foreknowledge* of God.

Paul, the *wise master builder*, masterfully uses *the births of Jacob and Esau from the Old Testament to help defend the New Testament doctrines of predestination and election, from the standpoint of grace and not from the standpoint of works* (1 Cor. 3:10). First, Paul lays the foundation *for the principle of election through grace* in *a promise* made to Abraham. "At this time will I come, and Sarah shall have a son" (Rom. 9:9). Why *does Paul begin with Abraham?* Because:

Predestination and election through grace can be traced directly to the promises God made to Abraham in Genesis chapters 12, 15, and 17.

The promises made to Abraham are the bedrock upon which **the doctrine of unconditional election** *is built.*

The Law vs. the Promise

Now to Abraham and his seed were the promises made. He saith not, And to seeds, as of many; but as of one, And to thy seed, which is Christ.

And this I say, that the covenant, that was confirmed before of God in Christ, the law, which was four hundred and thirty years after, cannot disannul, that it should make the promise of none effect.

For if the inheritance be of the law, it is no more of promise: but God gave it to Abraham by promise.

(Gal. 3:16-18)

We have already offered scriptural evidence that *Abraham was justified by faith before the offering of Isaac.* We have also shown that *Abraham was justified because he believed in the Lord and the promises God made to him* (Gen. 15:6; Rom. 4:3). Therefore, when we speak of the *New Covenant* of *Grace*, we are essentially referring *to the fulfillment of a promise God made to Abraham* (Gen. 12:1-3).

In the book of Galatians, Paul confirms the truth that we as believers in Jesus Christ ***are Abraham's seed***, and *heirs according* *to **the promise*** (Gal. 3:29). Paul makes it quite plain: *Our inheritance as believers is not of the law, but of promise.* This is very important because *there are basically two kinds of covenants in scripture—**Conditional** and **Unconditional.***

The Law—A Conditional Covenant

<u>A Conditional covenant</u>: *A contract or agreement in which God and man are obligated to each other to fulfill the requirements or conditions of the covenant. If man fails to keep his obligations under the covenant, God is not obligated to fulfill his part. An example of a conditional covenant is the* **Edenic covenant** (Gen. 2:16-17).

The Old Testament Law of Moses is a conditional covenant (Ex. 19:5, Lev. 26:1- 46). It requires *absolute obedience* in order for one to be justified or even blessed (Rom. 2:13). Why is this significant?

Many New Testament believers still live under the shadow of the law (Heb. 10:1). ***They believe they will only be blessed and receive God's favor if they are obedient.***

This is due to legalistic theology. Like Pharaoh and the taskmasters of the Egyptian bondage, *the law provides less* (straw) *and yet demands more* (bricks) than the children of Israel were able to fulfill (Ex. 5:10-19). Because of this:

Many believers are not free to serve God without the condemnation that comes from failure to live up to the demands of the law.

The truth is, however,

Believers are already blessed and enjoy God's favor—not on the basis of obedience** (works) **but simply on the basis of God's grace** (the free gift of his unmerited favor) **and the finished work of Christ on the cross alone (Jn. 19:30). In Christ Jesus, ***there is no condemnation***, because the believer is ***free*** (Gk. *eleutheroo,* meaning *exempt*) *from the law of sin and death* (Rom. 8:1-3).

Grace—An Unconditional Covenant

__*An Unconditional covenant*__: *A contract in which God and man are bound in agreement. God is obligated to fulfill certain promises He has made to man* ***without any condition or obligation*** *on the part of man, except to* ***believe in God's unconditional promise.***

What we want to stress here is that Paul said, ***the promises made to Abraham constituted a covenant*** (Gal. 3:16-17). It is this ***unconditional covenant*** *that causes* ***the blessing of Abraham to come upon the church*** *(Abraham's seed through Christ)* ***unconditionally*** *and provides for the salvation of the New Testament believer* (Gal. 3:14). ***Therefore, all favor, blessings, gifts, and callings flow to the believer by grace and not by works.***

The Abrahami;;c Covenant is therefore an unconditional covenant because it is based on an unconditional promise (Gen. 12: 1-3). Understanding this is ***essential*** to understanding the *theology of grace.*

In Thee Shall All the Families of the Earth Be Blessed

And I will make of thee a great nation, and I will bless thee, and make thy name great; and thou shalt be a blessing:

And I will bless them that bless thee, and curse him that curseth thee: and in thee shall all families of the earth be blessed.

(Gen. 12:2-3)

The New Testament promise of salvation by grace is an unconditional covenant because it is based on the unconditional promises made to Abraham.

It requires ***complete faith*** in ***the finished work of Jesus Christ*** in order for one to be *justified* (Gal. 2:16). *Another example of an unconditional covenant is the* ***Noahic Covenant*** *between God and Noah* (Gen. 9:8-17). You see, beloved,

Grace is not founded upon the obedience of the law, but upon the obedience and faith of Jesus Christ (Rom. 5:19; Gal. 2:16, 3:22).

Furthermore, many believers seem to forget or simply ignore the fact that *the law was* ***never given to the church as a covenant.*** *It was only meant to be* ***a teacher,*** *and* ***has nothing whatsoever*** *to do with* ***the election, justification, and preservation of the believer*** (Rom. 6:14; Gal. 3:24-25). *A serious problem still exists today however, in that many believers* ***have not*** *yet come to the understanding that:*

1) The promise *of the New Covenant of Grace* ***precedes*** *the Old Covenant by* ***430 years*** (Gal. 3:17).

2) The promise *of the New Covenant* ***supersedes*** *the Old Covenant law and* ***cannot be made void*** *or* ***nullified*** *by the law* (Gal. 3:17).

The New Covenant of ***Grace*** *therefore is* ***founded upon the unconditional promises God made to Abraham*** *in Genesis chapter 12,* and culminates in ***the seed*** (or offspring) that would descend from him. That seed is Christ Jesus!

In Genesis chapters 12, 26, and 28, we find that God *not only made an unconditional covenant with Abraham He also* ***confirmed the same promises to Isaac and Jacob*** (Gen. 12:1-3, 26:1-4, 28:13-15). The important thing here to remember is:

God made these promises to Abraham, Isaac, and Jacob apart from any prior action or works of righteousness on their part.

He simply declared in a promise, ***"I will"*** *do thus and so.* Paul beautifully teaches this in the book of Galatians. This is the *main difference* between a legalist and a grace believer where *the doctrine of election* is concerned.

The legalist believes that his works *(foreknown or otherwise)* ***are taken into account in the process of election. Whereas, the grace believer understands that his works*** *(foreknown or otherwise)* ***were not taken into account in the process of election.***

As believers, we are saved not according to our works but according to the promise of God. ***We are heirs of the same promise made to Abraham.*** We are *heirs of God and joint heirs with Christ* because, Paul said that ***the promises were made to Abraham and to his seed*** (Gal. 3:16, Rom. 8:17).

Calling and Election

Wherefore the rather, brethren, give diligence to make your calling and election sure: for if ye do these things, ye shall never fall:
(2 Pet. 1:10)

And we know that all things work together for good to them that love God, to them who are the called according to his purpose.
For whom he did foreknow, he also did predestinate to be conformed to the image of his Son, that he might be the firstborn among many brethren.
Moreover whom he did predestinate, them he also called: and whom he called, them he also justified: and whom he justified, them he also glorified.
(Rom. 8:28-30)

Who hath saved us, and called us with an holy calling, not according to our works, but according to his own purpose and grace, which was given us in Christ Jesus before the world began.
(2 Tim. 1:9)

Now that we have established that *the New Covenant can be linked directly to the Abrahamic Covenant*, and that ***the New Covenant is in itself an unconditional covenant,*** let us now focus on the aspects of *foreknowledge, predestination, and the election of the believer.*

The theology of doctrines such as foreknowledge, predestination, and election are very confusing and are not easy for some ministers to understand, much less to explain these truths to believers.

Although *most theologians agree that foreknowledge plays a part in God's electing and calling men to salvation, they disagree, however, as to* ***how foreknowledge relates to predestination.*** Does foreknowledge simply imply a *mere* ***knowing beforehand***, or does it involve something more?

I believe the doctrine of election is one of the most important and most difficult of Bible doctrines to grasp. This is true especially for the legalist, since in his theology:

The legalist cannot disassociate his works from the process of election and being saved by grace alone. Yet, how can it be said that the believer is saved by grace alone if his works are to be taken into account?

The Legalist and Election

It is the misunderstanding applied to the foreknowledge of God that makes it difficult for the legalist to grasp the doctrine of election without works.

The legalist believes that **God simply foreknows the works and choices** *of the believer beforehand (or in advance) and then He* ***calls the believer, knowing beforehand that the believer will choose Christ, obey the gospel, and be saved.*** *The believer is then responsible to* ***make his calling and election sure by living a holy life*** *of righteous works and by enduring unto the end* (2 Pet. 1:10). Thus, to the legalist:

The believer's election to salvation is conditioned upon the believer's receiving the gospel and living a life of obedience through righteous works.

This all of course makes sense to the legalist and seems reasonable. However, is it entirely scriptural?

The Grace Believer and Election

The grace believer, on the other hand, believes that God chooses the believer in Christ and predestines him to salvation

through grace without regard for any works of righteousness (foreknown or otherwise) on the part of the one saved.

Thus:

The believer's election to salvation is unconditional, since it is based on the believer hearing the gospel and placing absolute trust and confidence in the finished work accomplished by the obedience and sacrifice of Christ.

The legalist rejects the grace believer's view of election because he believes that *the grace believer contends that election through grace involves a violation of a person's sovereign free will to choose to be saved.* However, this is not possible since the very *choice or desire* to be saved is *placed within man by God Himself and is a direct response to the drawing invitation of the Holy Spirit as the goodness of God leads men to repent.* (Phil. 2:13; Rom. 2:4)

Let's look at what the scriptures really teach regarding calling and election. Are calling and election the same? In my opinion the answer is no. However, they are closely related. One presupposes the other.

1) Calling: *or vocation has to do with* **God's purpose in us** (Jn. 15:16; Eph. 1:4).

2) Election: *has to do with* **God's choosing us** *in order that he might fulfill that calling or purpose in us* (Rom. 8:29; 2 Tim. 1:9)

Both *calling* and *election* are *according to* ***His own purpose and grace*** and ***according to the good pleasure of His will*** (2 Tim. 1:9; Eph. 1:5). You see, the scriptures teach us that *God* "worketh all things after the counsel of his own will [or purpose]" (Eph. 1:11). *God's will encompasses God's good pleasure and purpose.*

One cannot separate God's will from God's purpose. *There could be no calling or election of the believer without there first existing a will (thelema) and a purpose (prothesis).* Both of which belong to God and *are pre-determined to be in Christ before the world began* (2 Tim. 1:9).

The divine prerogatives of *predestination and foreordination* are therefore both consistent with what the apostle Peter referred to as "the determinate counsel and foreknowledge of God" (Acts 2:23) or "God's prearranged plan" (Acts 2:23 *The New Living Translation*). This proves that:

The determinate counsel** (boule) **of God and the foreknowledge** (proginosko) **of God work together to bring to pass His eternal purposes in the universe.

As with God's will and purpose, one cannot easily separate *the determinate counsel* of God from God's *foreknowledge*, as they are *sewn or knit together* to manifest the purposes of God. In short:

God's purpose in the universe is predetermined and is foreknown by Him.

For example, as the crucifixion of Christ was *no accident*, but was ***according to the determinate counsel and foreknowledge of God, so*** also is ***the predestination and foreordination of those who are elected to salvation through grace and faith in Christ.*** *Nothing in God's eternal purpose is by chance—not* the rebellion of Lucifer (Satan), not the fall of Adam, not the crucifixion of Christ, or any other incident in eternity. This is also true of God's electing believers to salvation.

Believers are not randomly saved by chance, but by choice and by purpose.

However, *it is God's choice and God's purpose* (Jn. 15:16). It is *the purpose of God, which he hath purposed in himself* (Ehp. 1:4-9).

The Election of Grace

(For the children being not yet born, neither having done any good or evil, that the purpose of God according to election might stand, not of works, but of him that calleth;)

It was said unto her, The elder shall serve the younger.

As it is written, Jacob have I loved, but Esau have I hated.

(Rom. 9:11-13)

Even so then at this present time also there is a remnant according to ***the election of grace.***

And if by grace, then is it no more of works: otherwise grace is no more grace. But if it be of works, then is it no more grace: otherwise work is no more work.

(Rom. 11:5-6)

That ***God chooses us*** in the drama of redemption can be seen from ***the call of Abraham to the election of Isaac and Jacob*** (Israel) (Isa. 41:8, 44:1).

Each ***act of choice*** was made without regard for the ***merit*** of any of these men. *They were sought out and chosen simply that God might reveal His grace to the world in the person of His Son, Jesus Christ, and that He might be glorified therein.* So,

What role does foreknowledge actually play in calling and election?

Calling and election are different sides of the same coin. That is, the coin of God's *good pleasure and purpose*. Which, says the scripture; "he hath purposed in himself " (Eph. 1:9).

Foreknowledge therefore takes into account not only the knowing beforehand of election but also the calling and choosing beforehand.

However, in calling and choosing beforehand the important thing to remember is that:

In spite of the fact that works of obedience follow a believer's faith, those merits, or works of obedience of the one called and chosen, are not taken into account.

The Principle of Election Without Works

It is this aspect of election that is often ignored by the legalist. *This is the only way one can reconcile Paul's teaching that the believer's election can only be according to God's grace and not according to works* (Rom. 11:5). This is precisely what Paul declares in the book of Romans, chapter 9, in the election of Jacob and Esau.

Nowhere in scripture does it say that God takes into account the works of one chosen or elected to grace. In fact, it says the opposite.

A man's works are not considered in election.

The first reference to the principle of election without works is given by Paul in Romans 9:7.

"In Isaac Shall Thy Seed Be Called"

We see not only a knowing beforehand, but a choosing beforehand as well. The same is true of *Jacob* in Romans 9:11-12, proving a knowing and a choosing beforehand without regard for the works of the one foreknown and forechosen.

There is a calling *(kleæsis; an invitation)* according to the purpose *(prothesis; a setting forth*) of God (Rom 8:28). In this manner, *Abraham was the called according his purpose, or the setting forth of God. Abraham was given an invitation or calling according to the purpose God had set forth for the world.* Remember, when God called Abraham out of idolatry, Abraham was a sinner.

By faith, Abraham obeyed the voice of God, not knowing where he would end up (Heb. 11:8). Yet, we must understand that:

God did not choose Abraham because of his works. Abraham had done no works. God chose Abraham *apart from* his works. Yet, in his foreknowledge he declared of Abraham:

For I know him, that he will command his children and his household after him, and they shall keep the way of the LORD, to do justice and judgment; that the LORD may bring upon Abraham that which he hath spoken of him.

(Gen. 18:19)

This verse does not take away from the premise that ***Abraham and his seed were chosen by God without regard for their works*** *(which he foreknew). It simply means that* ***God did not choose them because of their works, but rather, apart from their works.***

That being the case, since the same unconditional promise was confirmed to all three, we must then conclude:

If God had chosen Abraham, Isaac, and Jacob on the basis of His foreknowledge of their works, this would then imply that God's un-conditional promise was actually conditional, when we know in fact it was not.

God said, *"For I know him."* The word *know* here is *Yada.* It means *to declare and* involves *a foreknowing centered around God's eternal purpose* (Gen. 18:19). *W.E. Vine says of this verse, "In Gen. 18:19 God says He knows Abraham; He cared for him in the sense that He chose him from among other men and saw to it that certain things happened to him. The emphasis is on the fact that God knew him intimately and personally."*

This is an example of *foreknowledge, predestination, and election working together to fulfill God's redemptive plan for the world.* In like manner, as God knew Abraham, he also knew Esau and Jacob.

Where Is Boasting Then?

Where is boasting then? It is excluded. By what law? of works? Nay: but by the law of faith.

(Rom. 3:27)

If God did not consider the works of Esau and Jacob in their calling and election, then we must also conclude that neither was Abraham's, Isaac's, yours, or mine. As stated previously,

God chose election according to grace so that no one could boast in his or her works!

God's choice of Jacob over Esau occurred before they were born: "…(For the children being not yet born, neither having done any good or evil,)"(Rom. 9:11). Paul makes it clear that *God's choice of Jacob over Esau was so that* "the purpose of God according to election might stand, not of works, but of him that calleth" so that none could boast (Rom. 9:10-11). Thus *the elder* (the law) shall *serve the younger* (grace). You see, as believers, "he hath chosen us in him before the foundation of the world" (Eph. 1:4).

God therefore calls the elect by grace and not by our works that the purpose of God according to election might stand. So then it (election) is "not of him that willeth, nor of him that runneth, but of God that sheweth mercy" (Rom. 9:16). It couldn't be any plainer. In summary, regardless of whatever else may be said about the *free will* of man and the *sovereign grace* of God, let us not forget that *election* is according to *the foreknowledge of God* (1 Pet. 1:2). This foreknowledge takes into account that man is saved only by God's grace and does nothing to commend himself to this grace wherein he stands justified by faith in Jesus Christ. Rather, it is God who commends himself toward us in that "while we were yet sinners, Christ died for us" (Rom. 5:8).

Through *sovereign grace,* God freely gave to man what he demanded of him through *the law—righteousness.* What man could not attain under the law, God provided for him under grace through faith. "For Christ is the end of the law for righteousness to every one that believeth" (Rom. 10:4). For Christ *is made unto us .. righteousness* (1 Cor. 1:30). And we are made the righteousness of God in him (2 Cor. 5:21).

PART IV

PRESERVATION & THE SECURITY OF THE BELIEVER

My sheep hear my voice, and I know them, and they follow me:

And I give unto them eternal life; and they shall never perish, neither shall any man pluck them out of my hand.

My Father, which gave them me, is greater than all; and no man is able to pluck them out of my Father's hand.

John 10:27-29

Preservation:

That act of God
whereby
He, through the
Holy Spirit and the blood of Jesus Christ,
seals, preserves, and keeps
the believer in Christ
in a state of redemptive grace,
thereby safeguarding the believer's salvation
unto the day of Jesus Christ.

14

Eternal Security

Jude, the servant of Jesus Christ, and brother of James, to them that are sanctified by God the Father, and ***preserved*** *in Jesus Christ, and called.*

(Jude 1, emphasis added)

And the Lord shall deliver me from every evil work, and will ***preserve*** *me unto his heavenly kingdom.*

(2 Tim. 4:18, emphasis added)

And grieve not the holy Spirit of God, whereby ye are ***sealed*** *unto the day of redemption.*

(Eph. 4:30, emphasis added)

Wherefore let them that suffer according to the will of God commit the keeping of their souls to him in well doing, as unto a faithful Creator.

(1 Pet. 4:19)

We shall now go in another direction and introduce a very difficult and controversial subject—the doctrine of *the eternal security of the believer.*

Is the security of the believer's salvation conditional or unconditional?

Here is where law and grace face their ultimate test. In doing so, we hope to shed some light and understanding in this area and provide some answers to some very important questions. Among them:

Can a believer ever lose his salvation and be eternally lost?

Is grace, the blood of Jesus, and the finished work of Calvary sufficient to guarantee the believer's security, or must one also rely upon legalism and human merit (one's own righteous works) to make the believer's salvation secure? It is the writer's position that:

The believer's security has nothing to do with the righteous works of the believer, and everything to do with the believer's enduring faith in the promise of God and God's ability to keep, preserve, and safeguard the believer's salvation.

The basis from which the believer's salvation is secure is his persevering enduring faith in the blood of Jesus Christ and His finished work at Calvary.

In fact, the Apostle Peter speaks of believers as those:

Who are ***kept by the power of God through faith*** *unto salvation ready to be revealed in the last time*

(1 Pet 1:5, emphasis added)

Interestingly, the Greek word for ***kept*** used is this verse is *phroureo*. It is a military term meaning:

To keep by guarding, or to keep under guard as with a garrison. It is used of *providing protection against the enemy and of blocking up every way of escape.*

Here we have a picture of ***the believer's salvation made secure because of God's ability to keep, guard and to protect the believer's salvation.*** In this verse, the Apostle Peter provides us with the following:

<u>*Three Important Aspects of the Security of the Believer*</u>

- *The* ***identity*** *of the one doing the keeping* ***(God)***
- *The* ***means*** *of the one being kept* ***(Power of God)***
- *The* ***condition*** *for being kept* ***(Faith)***

Notice the scripture *does not read—who are kept by the power of God through* ***works***, but rather it reads—*who are kept by the power of God through* ***faith***.

Arminianism and Calvinism

In matters of the security of the believer, there are *fundamentally two points of view.* Historically, there are essentially two theological camps resembling law and grace theology. We know them today as *Arminianism* and *Calvinism.* In my opinion, all believers lean *more or less* to one camp or the other. It is also common for some believers to embrace doctrine from each position.

One camp holds the view of *conditional* eternal security; the other holds the view of *unconditional* eternal security. However, these terms mean different things to different people depending on the perspective of their theology.

It is my position that there are two aspects of the believer's eternal security that must be considered and understood. They are the aspects of *perseverance and preservation.*

For the purposes of this work, I will attempt to show how the doctrines of *perseverance* and (or) *preservation* relate to each other and how they impact the security of the believer from the perspective of *grace theology* and *legalism.* This is essential in order to understand the basis from which the believer's salvation is made secure.

1) <u>Conditional Eternal Security</u>: The Arminian camp tends to embrace legalistic theology. Why?

Legalism places the responsibility of perseverance and the subsequent preservation of salvation on the part of the believer.

This means the believer's eternal security is *uncertain* since it is *conditioned upon God's acceptance of the believer's works of righteousness.*

In other words, if the believer perseveres in works of righteousness (lives a holy life that he deems is pleasing to God), *then he is preserved in Christ and will not lose his salvation.*

The downside of this position is that, *if the believer does not meet the standard for righteousness* (which is always subjective), *he will forfeit his salvation. In my opinion this view is very troubling, because if we, as the Pharisees, trust in ourselves that we are righteous, we are no different than the Mormons and Jehovah's Witnesses. We will not be saved because we trust in the merit of our own works of righteousness* (Lk. 18:9-14).

2) Unconditional Eternal Security: The Calvinistic camp tends to embrace *grace theology.* Why?

Grace theology places the responsibility of perseverance on the part of the believer, but the responsibility of preservation of the believer's salvation on the part of God.

However, the believer *perseveres in faith* ***in the blood*** and not in his works.

This means the believer's eternal security *is certain and unconditional since it has nothing to do with God's acceptance of the merit of the believer's works. It is based solely on the believer's persevering or* ***enduring faith*** *in the blood atonement and the finished work of Christ alone. In other words:*

If the believer perseveres in faith in Jesus Christ and His finished work of atonement, his salvation is eternally secure.

Perseverance and Preservation

In my studies over the years, I have discovered (to my dismay) that both Arminians and Calvinists have emphasized the single aspect of *perseverance* in regards to the security of the believer's salvation.

I consider myself to be neither totally Arminian nor Calvinist. I am however alarmed that those who believe in salvation by *grace* alone would stress the theological use of the term *perseverance* but also neglect the Bible's teaching in the area of the *preservation* of the believer. I suspect that this could be due to the common use of the term *preservation* elsewhere in theology.

For purposes of this work, I would like to offer the following definition of the biblical context of *preservation* as it pertains to the security of the believer.

Preservation: *That act of God whereby He through faith, the Holy Spirit, and the blood of Jesus Christ,* ***seals, preserves*** *and* ***keeps*** *the believer in Christ in a state of redemptive grace—thereby* ***safeguarding*** *the believer's salvation unto the day of Jesus Christ.*

Can the believer build a solid scriptural case for the aspect of preservation in matters of the believer's security in addition to the doctrine of perseverance? The answer is yes. *At least two* New *Testament writers* ***directly use*** *the words* ***preserve*** *or* ***preserved*** *in their writings—****Paul and Jude*** (1 Thess. 5:23; 2 Tim. 4:18; Jude 1). I believe:

It is therefore scriptural for believers to think of the security of the believer in terms of both perseverance and preservation.

In the matter of the security of their salvation, ***believers are to persevere in faith*** (or trust) ***in the finished work of Calvary.*** This is the ***only basis*** of the believer's eternal security and preservation in Christ (1 Pet. 1:5).

He That Endureth To the End

But he that shall endure unto the end, the same shall be saved.
(Matt. 24:13)

Someone may be wondering, "Well, what about Matthew 24:13?" In my opinion this is one of the most often quoted scriptures of the legalist when referring to the doctrine of *perseverance.*

While it is true that the scriptures do declare, *"He that shall endure unto the end, the same shall be saved,"* it is also true that ***this scripture, when understood and applied in its proper context, does not pertain to the security of the believer at all.*** Rather, it pertains to the period in prophecy yet to come, referred to as the ***tribulation,*** or ***the time of Jacob's trouble*** (Matt. 24:21; Jer. 30:7).

The legalist has sought refuge in this and similar verses that speak of enduring to the end (perseverance) or of overcoming, to support their teaching of ***perpetuating and maintaining righteousness through works.*** Essentially, what this verse has come to mean to the legalist and those who embrace Arminian theology and conditional eternal security is that,

In order to be saved, one must live a victorious life above sin and steadfastly maintain a life of faith evidenced by practical holiness, until death or the rapture, whichever comes first.

The consequence, of course, if one does not *endure* or persevere to the end *in this manner* is he or she will ultimately ***lose*** *their* salvation. However, it is the fear of losing his ***free gift*** of salvation that motivates the legalist to ***earn or work his way to heaven through human merit*** (Rom. 5:15-18). Here again, we must take strong issue with the legalist.

A Dispensational Point Of View

As stated before, when *New Testament scriptures are viewed from the vantage point of Sinai and not from Calvary, serious doctrinal problems will inevitably ensue.* This is why a basic understanding of *dispensational theology* is essential. From a dispensational point of view,

The scripture in Matthew 24:13 does not even apply to the church at all, but to the nation of Israel during the time of the tribulation.

This chapter and other related passages pertain only to those Israelites (Jewish believers) who will *endure the tribulation*, or *"the time of Jacob's trouble."*

The message here is that even *during a time of severe persecution, testing, and trial, God will* **preserve** *the nation of Israel from being destroyed by the Anti-Christ and his armies* (Isa. 31:5). At the same time, *He will save a remnant of Jewish believers who will preach* **the gospel of the kingdom** *proclaiming that, "the King is coming, the King is coming!"*

Eschatology (the study of end time events) is not my strong point. I know many believers differ on this point and hold to either *a pre-tribulation, mid-tribulation, or post-tribulation* rapture theory.

Many noted Bible scholars believe ***the church will be absent during the time of Jacob's trouble and are present at the marriage supper of the Lamb, and therefore cannot be the elect tribulation saints spoken of in this chapter*** (Matt. 24:22,31; Rev. 19:7-9).

In my opinion, if one holds a *pre-tribulation rapture* view, then this scripture *cannot* apply to the church at all. One would have to hold a *mid-tribulation or post tribulation rapture* view in order for the *elect* in this verse to be the church. However, the Bible teaches that:

There are two elect groups in scripture:

- ***The Nation of Israel***: God's ***elect according to race*** (Isa. 45:4)
- ***The Church***: *God's* ***elect according to grace*** (Rom. 8:33)

Often in prophecy, they are mistaken one for the other. Many legalists have not recognized this distinction when teaching *perseverance,* and misunderstanding and false teaching is perpetuated.

If I understand my Bible correctly, *there will be* ***144,000 elect Israelites*** *saved (and possibly martyred) during the tribulation. These will prepare the nation for the coming of the literal, visible Second Coming of Jesus Christ as KING OF KINGS, AND LORD OF LORDS to establish his millennial kingdom here on earth* (Rev. 7:4, 19:16).

The strongest evidence of this comes from the text of Matthew, chapter 24 itself. References to ***the gospel of the kingdom, a restored Jewish temple in Jerusalem, the abomination of desolation standing in the holy place, a flight on the Sabbath, etc., could pertain only to Jewish believers during the tribulation period.*** In my opinion, Matthew 24:13 is just for them.

Saved To Be Saved?

When I first heard of the doctrine of *eternal security,* it was presented to me as the teaching of *"once saved, always saved."* I thought, *how silly—everybody knows that in order to get to heaven you've got to be good. Only good people go to heaven, right?* Wrong!

The truth of the matter is—only blood-washed people go to heaven!

When I first came to the Lord at the young age of seventeen, my pastor (the most godly man I ever met) told me of the necessity of the saints ***"enduring unto the end."*** I will never forget his words: ***"We are saved to be saved."*** He then explained that *salvation is a lifetime process.* It begins at the *New Birth* and ends at *death* or the *rapture.*

Between regeneration and glorification is a corresponding ***work*** *or* ***process*** *called* ***sanctification****, which manifests itself through a life of personal holiness.* (We shall expound on this process later). This is the only way to *guarantee* that the saved and sanctified soul is sure to secure for himself a mansion in heaven.

Of course, if one is a *legalist* and believes in salvation through *human merit,* this reasoning makes perfect sense. However, is this reasoning compatible with being saved by *grace* alone? I think not. The apostle Paul confronted this kind of reasoning in his epistle to the church in *Galatia.* In writing to combat *legalism among the Galatians*, Paul asked them this question:

Are ye so foolish? having begun in the ***Spirit,*** *are ye now made perfect by the* ***flesh****?*

(Gal. 3:3, emphasis added)

My question therefore to the legalist is, "Were you *saved by grace yesterday only to be saved by works today?*" Well, what happens when your todays become your yesterdays? Like others we have studied, you ***will have then departed from the principle of salvation by grace to embrace the principle of salvation by works.*** As stated earlier,

Legalism is any religious system that establishes righteousness through works.

The legalist sincerely believes he ***enters*** the church by faith in the blood, but ***afterwards*** he initiates ***a campaign of faith in his works so he may be righteous enough to enter heaven.*** Therefore,

- *The legalist believes he will go to heaven only if he maintains a certain standard of righteousness through human merit* (holy living).

- *The legalist believes he will forfeit his salvation and be eternally lost if he does not.*

He That Overcometh

Another Arminian stronghold is found in the book of Revelation. It speaks of believers overcoming.

He that overcometh, the same shall be clothed in white raiment; and I will not blot out his name out of the book of life, but I will confess his name before my Father, and before his angels.
(Rev. 3:5)

For many years as a legalist, I used this scripture to refute the doctrine of unconditional eternal security. *This scripture appeared to me to be a threat and a plain warning to believers against backsliding and worldly living.* I preached this verse for years to carnal church members, *using fear and intimidation to manipulate them into godly living.* It seemed to me that God was plainly saying:

"If you don't overcome sin, the world, and the devil, you will

not be clothed in white raiment, and I will erase your name from the book of life."

Then one day the Holy Spirit allowed me to see that this verse is not a threat at all, but a precious promise. Until then, I had always interpreted this scripture from the vantage point of Sinai. However, when I began to view this scripture from the vantage point of Calvary, *I realized that I am already an overcomer, not because of my works, but because I am in Christ Jesus!*

Furthermore, I realized that because I am an overcomer through Christ, He will never blot out my name from the book of life! What a precious promise! With this new understanding my relationship with God went from the *fear and insecurity wrought by legalism*, to the *complete assurance and absolute trust all believers enjoy through grace.* Especially when one considers that,

As believers, we do not overcome sin, the world, and Satan by our righteous works. We overcome sin, the world, and Satan by the word of our testimony (the confession of our faith) ***and by the blood of the Lamb*** (Rom. 10:9-10; Rev. 12:11).

The *book of Revelation* is rich in symbolism. *Even the white raiment promised to the believer is significant and testifies to the fact that the principles of substitution and atonement can be found in all ages and dispensations* (Rev. 3:5). These *holy* garments are only ***given*** to the redeemed of all ages and dispensations. *Is this the same white raiment alluded to elsewhere in Revelation, chapters 7 and 19?* I believe it is.

And I said unto him, Sir, thou knowest. And he said to me, These are they which came out of great tribulation, and have washed their robes, and made them white in the ***blood of the Lamb****.*

(Rev. 7:14, emphasis added)

And to her was granted that she should be arrayed in fine linen, clean and white: for the fine linen is the righteousness of saints.

(Rev. 19:8)

As we interpret these verses from the vantage point of Calvary and the *grace* of God, we must conclude that ***the righteousness of saints*** *is none other than the* **imputed** *righteousness of Jesus Christ.* ***This righteousness is imputed to the believer through faith in His blood, not through human merit.*** It is represented here as *the fine linen clean and white, and the robes washed in the* ***blood*** *of the* ***Lamb***. We know this because the garments are ***promised*** *and* ***furnished*** to the believer by the Lord himself (Rev. 3:5).

What a beautiful picture of the substitution and atonement wrought through the finished work of Calvary.

- ***The Lamb*** *speaks of Christ's work of* ***substitution.***
- ***The blood*** *speaks of Christ's work of* ***atonement.***

These truths only become clear when we interpret the scriptures from Calvary and not from Sinai. There is no room here for the believer to boast in his own works of righteousness. Therefore,

Arminian theology is largely built upon a foundation of salvation based upon human merit (works). ***It is not compatible with salvation by grace and is not consistent with the principles of substitution and atonement. Arminian theology is nothing less than legalism masquerading as salvation through grace.***

Like Jacob who deceived his father Isaac,

Legalism supplants the gift of righteousness with righteousness through works and deceives those who trust in its falsehood (Rom. 5:17).

Indeed, when we examine it closely, "…the voice is Jacob's voice, but the hands are the hands of Esau" (Gen. 27:22).

Whosoever Believeth in Him

For God so loved the world, that he gave his only begotten Son, ***that whosoever believeth in him*** *should not perish, but have*

everlasting life.

(Jn. 3:16, emphasis added)

Everything that we have said thus far about the security of the believer has led us to conclude that we must make the following distinction between *conditional* and *unconditional* eternal security.

- *The preservation of the believer's salvation is* ***unconditional*** *concerning the believer's works of merit* (whether good or bad). *However, it is also fair to say*:

- *The preservation of the believer's salvation is* ***conditional*** *in that it requires complete trust and genuine enduring faith in Jesus Christ and his finished work of atonement.*

The salvation *covenant* can only exist between God and man *based on* the believer's enduring faith in Jesus Christ and His finished work. The scripture says, *He that believeth.* This can and should be interpreted as *He that continues to believe.*

It is on the basis of repentance and faith that the believer's debt of sin (past, present and future) has been canceled by the blood of Jesus and is not taken into account.

I believe that it is therefore fair to say,

A believer who perseveres in faith in this manner can never be eternally lost as long as he places absolute trust in Christ and not in his own works of righteousness.

Regardless of his level of *maturity* or degree of *victory* in his life, *in the end he shall be saved* "yet so as by fire" (1 Cor. 3:15). This subject will be covered later in more detail.

However, I believe it is also fair and necessary to qualify what constitutes the definition of *a believer.*

- *A believer* is not one who merely *professes* salvation, but one who *possesses* salvation through *a genuine New*

Birth experience.

- *A believer* is one who places *absolute trust* in the merit of the shed blood of Jesus Christ and His finished work of atonement at Calvary as the basis for his salvation.

- *A believer* must not only *confess with his mouth* the Lord Jesus, he must also *believe in his heart* in order to be genuinely saved (Rom. 10: 9-10). Furthermore,

- *A believer* must persevere in faith. That is, he must *continue* to believe in the same manner—by confession and possession until Jesus comes.

In conclusion, I may not understand the theology of *universal vs. limited atonement, supralapsarianism vs. sublapsarianism, conditional vs. unconditional election,* or the mysteries of *sovereign grace.* However, I do know one thing.

Everyday when I awaken, something within me says, *I want to be more like Jesus.* I am not trying to be *good enough* to make it in. I am trying to become more like Jesus.

I am saved by grace—I walk by faith—I confess my sin and repent when I stumble. As a believer, as long as I place my faith in the blood of Jesus, I have the assurance of God's Word that I can never be lost.

Holiness:

The state of grace
into which the believer in Christ
is called, wherein
he is set apart in Christ,
separated from sin,
and dedicated to the glory
and purposes of God.

15

The Doctrine of Holiness

Follow peace with all men, and holiness, without which no man shall see the Lord:

(Heb. 12:14)

A man out tending his father-in-law's business one day was suddenly distracted by an event so incredible and so unbelievable that he left his charge to view an unusual sight. A bush was on fire. There was nothing special about this bush. It was just a common, ordinary, desert variety bush, yet it was not being burned up in the least. As the man moved cautiously forward to investigate, someone called his name from the midst of the bush, *"Moses, Moses."* The one who called to him from the bush identified himself *as the God of Abraham, the God of Isaac, and the God of Jacob* (Ex. 3:6).

With the background of this event in mind, I would like to share my thoughts on *the doctrine of holiness*. I realize that much could be written on the subject of holiness. I would like to add my contribution. First, I would like to *distinguish the difference between holiness as a state of being and holiness as a lifestyle.* I will then focus on an often-overlooked aspect of holiness—*the pursuit of the nature and character of Jesus Christ.*

Holiness, A State of Being

And he said, Draw not nigh hither: put off thy shoes from off thy feet, for the place whereon thou standest is holy ground.

(Ex. 3:5)

Holiness is first—a state of being. Merriam-Webster's Dictionary defines *holiness* as:

> ***1)*** *The quality or state of being holy.* Anyone or anything that God *chooses* to use for His purpose can be *made* holy. In the Old Testament, *people, places, and things are found holy and are set apart, separated, and dedicated to Jehovah.*

A) Israel is called God's *holy people* (Deut. 7:6).
B) Jerusalem is called the *holy city* (Isa. 52:1).
C) ***The Levites, the tabernacle,*** *and* ***all the vessels of the sanctuary*** *are said to be holy* (2 Chron. 5:5,23:6).

Even ***the ground Moses stood upon*** in the presence of God was *holy* (*Heb. qo'desh*) (Ex 3:5). Unlike the bush that burned with fire, *the ground was not a living thing. It had no being, lifestyle, or character of its own.* Yet, *the ground was for this moment and purpose in time declared to be holy.* Why? Because from this place God chose to manifest *his will* and communicate *his purpose* to his servant Moses.

While Moses, the murderer and the fugitive from justice stood upon this hallowed ground, *this ground in turn sanctified Moses*, giving an un-holy man a place to stand and to speak in the presence of a holy God. *This is the first instance of the word "holy" being used in the Bible.*

With a single act of consecration (the removing of his shoes), there Moses stood, barefoot in the presence of a holy God. From that day forward, Moses, the murderer and fugitive from justice, found *favor* with God and became God's *holy messenger* and *a deliverer* to a nation who would someday bring forth *the Savior* of the world. Moses would return to this sacred place, ascend the *holy mountain* of God (Sinai) and receive the *holy commandments* engraved upon two tablets of stone, written with *the finger of God* (Ex. 31:18).

Holiness, A Lifestyle

But as he which hath called you is holy, so be ye holy in all manner of conversation;
Because it is written, Be ye holy; for I am holy.
(1 Pet. 1:15,16)

Holiness is a ***lifestyle*** as well as ***a state of being.*** Let me state for the record that *I believe in the doctrine of holiness. I believe in holy living and that believers should endeavor to live a lifestyle* (in word and deed) *that will bring glory to God* (1 Cor. 10:31). However, I believe that,

All believers are first holy in standing through the finished work of Christ.

In the New Testament, believers are called *saints* (*Gk. hagios*), *which means, sanctified or holy ones* (Rom 1:7). Believers are also called *a royal priesthood, an holy nation, and a peculiar people* (1 Pet. 2:9; Tit. 2:14).

Because God is holy, and because of their holy standing, believers are called to a lifestyle of holiness (1 Pet. 1:15; 1 Thess. 4:7).

Some think believers are called to be *holy* in order to be separate from sin. This is, of course, *true* and *important.* However, there is a more important reason. That is,

Believers are called to be holy in order to fulfill God's purpose for which they have been called in Christ.

In order to fulfill that *purpose*, they must ensue ***a lifestyle of separation and dedication to the purpose or purposes for which God has called them.***

The Three Aspects of Holiness

There are three primary aspects of holiness. They are ***sanctifi-***

cation, separation, and dedication.

- *To be holy is to be* ***sanctified*** *or* ***set apart*** *in and for Christ.*

- *To be holy is to be* ***separated*** *from that which is sinful or profane.*

- *To be holy is to be* ***dedicated*** *or* ***consecrated*** *unto the purposes of God.*

All New Testament believers are therefore *sanctified* (set apart) *in Christ, separated from sin, and dedicated or consecrated to the purposes of God and the service of Christ.* Having this in mind, I would like to offer the following definition of holiness:

<u>Holiness</u>: ***The state of grace*** *into which the believer in Christ is called wherein he is* ***set apart*** *in Christ,* ***separated from*** *sin, and* ***dedicated to*** *the glory and purposes of God.*

That being said, it is time we all took another look at *the doctrine of holiness. Some, I am afraid, are not getting the point and confusing legalism with holiness.* Let me say, it is not my desire or intent to be judgmental or critical of my brethren. I do not want to come across as arrogant or self-righteous. I pray I will not be perceived in this manner. However, there are things I must say in order to bring forth the truth, as I understand it.

Much of what I hear being taught in the name of holiness is not (in my opinion) *holiness at all, but legalism.* Often *holiness* is preached with *a self-righteous, judgmental, "holier than thou spirit"* trying to pawn itself off to the *Body of Christ* and the world as the ***spirit of holiness*** (Isa. 65:5; Rom. 1:4).

We have already said *that holiness is a lifestyle that all believers should pursue. What better lifestyle to pursue than the* ***nature*** *and* ***character*** *of our Lord Jesus Christ.* The Bible says that Christ was "holy, harmless, undefiled, separate from sinners" (Heb.7:26). He attended weddings, funerals, feasts, dinners, and so forth. Yet, we know that ***Christ loved sinners.***

Unlike the *Pharisees* who *had the wrong idea about holiness and separated themselves from the company of sinners*, we know that *Christ walked among sinners, ate, drank and abode with them. Yet, He did not partake in their sins.*

Without compromising His personal holiness, Christ allowed His life to touch others in such a way that they could see the love, compassion, and mercy of the Father through His life, words, and deeds. In this manner, Christ lived a holy life. This is the lifestyle to which the believer is called.

True Holiness

And that ye put on the new man, which after God is created in righteousness and true holiness.

(Eph. 4:24)

Everyone that comes preaching in the name of *holiness* is not necessarily preaching holiness. The Bible speaks about *true holiness* (Eph. 4:24). *If there is true holiness, then there must also be false holiness, which is not according to truth.* **Legalism is not true holiness.**

True holiness is the work of the Holy Spirit in the life of the believer. Legalism is the work of man.

I will never accept the premise that a man can become holy through any means available to him.

One cannot become holy through good works. Only God Almighty can make a believer holy through the sanctifying agencies of the Holy Spirit. As long as man relegates the work of holiness to human effort and the result of holiness to human merit, he will be forever ensnared in the bramble of legalism.

How Is the Believer Sanctified?

The following agencies are used by God the Father to perfect sanctification in the life of the believer (Jude 1). *Each agency has a part in* ***affecting, ensuring, safeguarding, or preserving*** *the* *believer's eternal salvation. The believer is sanctified:*

- *By the* ***Holy Spirit*** (Rom. 15:16; 2 Thess. 2:13; 1 Pet 1:1)
- *By the* **Word of God** (Jn. 17:17; Eph. 5:26)
- *By the* ***offering of the body of Jesus*** (Heb. 10:10)
- *By* ***faith*** *in Christ Jesus* (Acts 26:18)
- *By* ***the blood*** *of Jesus Christ* (Heb. 13:12)
- *By* ***the name*** *of Jesus Christ* (1 Cor. 6:11)

True holiness is not the end result of conforming to a higher ***religious standard, code of conduct,*** *or* ***a list of rules of do's and don'ts****. True holiness has nothing whatsoever to do with women wearing pants, long dresses, make-up and jewelry. True holiness has nothing whatsoever to do with whether believers should attend movie theatres or own television sets.*

So, where do all these legalistic rules come from? In my opinion, *many preachers have the wrong idea about holiness.* Like modern day *Pharisees*, they approach *holiness* from the vantage point of Sinai, preaching, "*Touch not; taste not; handle not.*" The apostle Paul says these doctrines are nothing but *the commandments and doctrines of men* (Col. 21-22).

True holiness has to do with the believer being sanctified in Christ, and with Christ being sanctified daily in the life of the believer. As the believer is sanctified in Christ, Christ can then be sanctified in the life of the believer (Eph. 4:24).

The end result of true holiness is that the world will see Christ. If this is true, this would shed some light on the passage found in Hebrews 12:14 which reads:

Follow peace with all men, and holiness, without which no man shall see the Lord.

This is one of the most often abused scriptures among legalists when teaching *holiness. Does this scripture simply mean that without a lifestyle of peace and holiness no man* (sinners or believers) *will ever physically and visibly see the Lord?* Yes, I would agree, but only in a narrow sense is this true. I believe this verse could have a *two-fold* meaning.

1) ***Holiness*** *is essential in order for* ***the believer to see the Lord*** *at His coming.*

2) ***Holiness*** *is essential in order for* ***a lost world to see the Lord*** *in the life of the believer.*

In a broader sense, Hebrews 12:14 also implies that, *no* man (saved or unsaved) *shall see Christ in the life of the believer unless the believer lives a life of personal holiness.* That's a stretch, you say? Not really—here's why:

The scriptures tell us that all men shall see God at the time of the judgment, whether saved or not. Did not the writer to the Hebrews say that "it is appointed unto men once to die, but after this the judgment:" (Heb. 9:27)? *Will not all men literally see the Lord at either the judgment seat of Christ or the great white throne judgment to give account of themselves* (2 Cor. 5:10; Rev 20:12)? *If the saved shall see the Lord and give account of themselves, shall not the unsaved also give account of themselves at the throne of judgment* (Lk. 16:2; Rom. 14:11)?

Did not the apostle Paul write *that every knee should bow and every tongue should confess that Jesus Christ is Lord* (Phil. 2:10-11)? Will we not all bow before the Lord Himself (Isa. 45:23)? If no man shall see the Lord without holiness, then how can this scripture be fulfilled?

Did not the apostle John write, *And I saw the dead, small and great, stand before God; and the books were opened: and another book was opened, which is the book of life: and the dead were judged out of those things which were written in the books, according to their works* (Rev. 20:12)? If no man shall see the Lord without holiness, then how can the dead, small and great, stand before God, be judged and then cast into the lake of fire (Rev. 20:15)?

A narrow interpretation of Hebrews 12:14 would not allow a sinner (a lost, unholy person) to stand before God at the judgment. So, there must be a broader meaning here.

I once had a man in a congregation I served as pastor who was teaching from Hebrews 12:14. He explained this verse like this:

"The only Jesus that the world will ever see is the Jesus they will see in you and me."

I believe Brother Melvin was right. If we do not follow peace and holiness, *no man will see the Lord.* Why follow *peace and holiness?* ***Because peace and holiness are the nature and character of Christ.*** So, the broader interpretation of this scripture reveals:

- *To live holy is* ***to live Christ-like.***
- *To live Christ-like is* ***to live a lifestyle*** *that reflects the* ***nature*** *and* ***character*** *of Christ.*

As believers, we are holy in a practical sense only to the degree that men can see Jesus Christ in us. If the world cannot see Christ reflected in your life and mine, then we are holy in our state of being and not in our manner of living.

We are merely playing the Pharisee's game of *hypocrisy and deceit* (Rom. 8:29; Gal. 4:19).

The Pentecostal-Holiness Movement

Merriam-Webster's Dictionary also defines *holiness* as:

2) *Emphasizing the doctrine of the second blessing; specifically: of or relating to a perfectionist movement arising in U.S. Protestantism in the late 19th century.*

I want to speak briefly on the subject of *legalism and the 20th century Pentecostal-Holiness movement.* The Pentecostal-Holiness movement began at the turn of the century around 1901. *The Pentecostal-Holiness movement claims to be a progression of the Protestant Reformation and claims to espouse the principle of justification by faith.* Historically, this is so. However, when one examines the movement's doctrines closely, one finds strong evidence that the *Pentecostal-Holiness movement* as a whole is in fact *a stronghold of legalism.*

The Pentecostal-Holiness movement leans heavily toward the principle of righteousness through human merit (works) as evidenced by its extreme views on the doctrines of sanctification, personal holiness, and perseverance.

It is how these doctrines affect their position of the conditional security of the believer that we are now concerned. Since much of my background and experience is in *Pentecostal* and *Holiness* churches, I feel I must now address them in particular.

All of my life I have been a *Pentecostal*. Because of the emphasis on the *"baptism with the Holy Spirit"* evidenced by *speaking with other tongues* and being *"Spirit filled,"* ***there is and always has been a tremendous anointing on the Pentecostal movement.*** I learned how to pray, preach, and worship through my Pentecostal heritage. In my opinion,

The Pentecostal movement has impacted 20th century Christianity and theology more than any other.

Most of the evangelistic preaching and teaching done from both television and radio is from the pulpits of Pentecostal and Charismatic ministries. However, I am also grieved to say that for the most part,

The Pentecostal movement has fallen prey to the seduction of legalism and contributes to its proliferation throughout the Body of Christ.

A little known fact among some Pentecostals and Charismatics is that,

The roots and doctrine of the holiness movement as espoused by most modern day Pentecostal and Charismatic circles are Arminian in origin and can be traced to the Nazarene and Methodist holiness movements of the 18th and 19th centuries.

From there, they can be traced to the Anglican Church of England, and from there to Roman Catholicism.

Furthermore,

Pentecostal theology is not in accordance with that of Martin Luther and his reformation teaching of justification by faith. Being Arminian in scope, it is therefore divergent from that of modern day reformed churches. The modern day Pentecostal movement has a rich and distinctly legalistic heritage, which cannot be refuted or denied.

That being said, we are now ready to examine the Pentecostal doctrine of holiness as it relates to the preservation of the believer.

"Saved, Sanctified, And Filled With the Holy Ghost"

Early Pentecostals struggled with the teaching of sanctification (holiness) and around *1911* were divided into *two camps.*

1) Those who believed in what was then called *"the second blessing"* held that ***sanctification occurred instantaneously*** ***as a second work of grace*** *after conversion and prior to the baptism with the Holy Ghost* (evidenced by speaking with other tongues). They began use of the phrase, *"saved, sanctified, and filled with the Holy Ghost"* among Pentecostals.

2) Those who believed that ***sanctification was the progressive work of grace*** *that began at conversion and spanned one's lifetime.* This teaching was *known among Pentecostals as "the finished work of Christ."*

These differences of doctrine caused much confusion and animosity within the Pentecostal community. This goes to show that even *at this time in history, the Holy Spirit was endeavoring to bring understanding to the Body of Christ in this area.*

It seems that legalism had such *a stronghold* that the message of ***the finished work of Calvary*** (as believed by grace believers today)

was never brought to maturity within the Pentecostal movement. Unfortunately,

> *Both Pentecostal camps essentially remain Arminian in theology, since they also hold the view that* ***a believer can lose his salvation if he fails to live a sanctified life as defined by their particular standard or doctrine of holiness.***

Although I consider myself a *reformed Pentecostal,* I am neither a *Calvinist* nor an *Arminian.* I find both camps have good and bad points, the truth resting somewhere in the middle. It is my position that,

> ***The sanctification of the believer is both an instantaneous and progressive work of God's redemptive grace and is accomplished and made possible only because of the finished work of Christ at Calvary.***

One of the reasons why the Pentecostal movement continues to be ensnared in legalism is because *it has relegated holiness teaching to an external code of righteousness through human merit,* rather than *the pursuit of the character of Christ.* In pursuit of what they interpreted sanctification and holiness to be, many churches and church organizations attempted to ***legislate holiness,*** and *devised rules* to govern the conduct of their members. These rules were often referred to as *"holiness standards."* While *they based some of these rules or holiness standards on scriptures or principles found in the Bible, many of the rules, however, cannot be found in the Bible.*

Issues that were not *expressly* dealt with in scripture were left to *the personal judgment and discretion of church leaders.* In many cases, *individual scriptures are taken out of their biblical context, spiritualized, and given new meanings and applications to suit whatever conduct they desired members to conform to.*

Some examples that come to mind are whether or not *women should be permitted to wear pants, make-up, jewelry, panty hose, allowed to cut their hair, or even shave their legs. Men are required to cut their hair and are forbidden to wear mustaches or beards.* While these may sound trivial and in some cases downright silly, *entire organizations have split and churches have broken fellowship because of these, and a host of other man-made rules* that have little or nothing to do with *true holiness.*

Other issues do not arise from matters of dress but from *misapplication of Old Testament scriptures that include whether believers should go to church on Saturday or Sunday, or whether or not believers should eat pork. Even tithing* (and I do believe in tithing) *has been mishandled and presented in a legalistic manner.*

Within the Body of Christ, many believers are also caught in the mire of legalism. They are *sincere, trusting, and obedient saints who only want to serve God and do those things that are pleasing in His sight.* However, they are victims of men who do not have a clue about what true holiness is. It is the writer's opinion that:

Legalism has been very destructive to the Body of Christ and is responsible for most of the disunity in the church today.

The attempt to legislate holiness has caused the Pentecostal movement to wallow in the mire of legalism. Within the *movement,* questions surrounding *how to define the nature of the Godhead, the essentiality and formula of water baptism, and speaking in tongues created strife and* caused brethren to *separate and break fellowship with one another.*

Because they did not see eye to eye in matters of holiness, some have caused much harm to the *Body of Christ* and have *withheld fellowship* from other believers simply *because they did not agree in matters of holiness.* Outside of the movement, issues *concerning keeping the Sabbath, baptism, and dietary issues continue to fragment the Body of Christ at large.* This proves that:

Legalism does not unify or bring oneness to the Body of Christ. It divides believers and brings more darkness and bondage.

Today, by the grace of God, *some Pentecostal and Charismatic groups are retreating from attitudes and positions they used to hold and are trying to abandon legalism* and embrace a more scriptural view of *the doctrine of holiness.* However, this shift is seen by the legalist as *compromise* and *worldliness.*

Rather than preaching against the personal use of *make-up and jewelry,* should we not rather focus on *developing the nature and character of Christ as the goal of personal holiness?* The Apostle Peter exhorts believers to give attention *to the* ***inner work*** *of holiness rather than focusing on the exterior or outward appearance.*

> *Whose adorning* ***let it not be*** *that* ***outward adorning*** *of plaiting the hair, and of wearing of gold, or of putting on of apparel; But* ***let it be the hidden man of the heart,*** *in that which is not corruptible, even the ornament of a meek and quiet spirit, which is in the sight of God of great price.*
>
> (1 Pet. 3:3-4, emphasis added).

Jesus warned against the hypocrisy of making an external profession of holiness when he rebuked the Pharisees, saying,

> *Woe unto you, scribes and Pharisees, hypocrites!* ***for ye make clean the outside*** *of the cup and of the platter,* ***but within*** *they are full of extortion and excess.*
>
> *Thou blind Pharisee,* ***cleanse first that which is within*** *the cup and platter, that the outside of them may be clean also.*
>
> *Woe unto you, scribes and Pharisees, hypocrites! for ye are like unto whited sepulchres, which indeed* ***appear beautiful outward,*** *but are* ***within full of dead men's bones, and of all uncleanness.***
>
> *Even so ye also outwardly appear righteous unto men, but* ***within ye are full of hypocrisy and iniquity.***
>
> (Matt. 23:25-28, emphasis added)

It is my opinion that a lifestyle of personal holiness is an outward manifestation of the inward work of the Holy Spirit.

- ***<u>Inwardly</u>:*** *holiness is* ***the work of the Holy Spirit*** *in the life of the believer bringing forth the* ***fruit of the Spirit*** *and the* ***character*** *of our Lord.*

  - ***<u>Outwardly</u>***: *holiness is* ***any action or conduct*** *on the part of the believer that* ***reveals*** *or causes the* ***nature and***

***character of Jesus to be seen** by the world.*

Sanctified Wholly

And the very God of peace sanctify you wholly; and I pray God your whole spirit and soul and body be preserved blameless unto the coming of our Lord Jesus Christ.

(1 Thess. 5:23)

And the LORD God formed man of the dust of the ground, and breathed into his nostrils the breath of life; and man became a living soul.

(Gen. 2:7)

As a finished work of grace through the *free gift* of God's unmerited favor, salvation also includes *the finished work of sanctification*. The believer is *sanctified* through various means. However, it is important to understand that:

Salvation and sanctification occur in three distinct dimensions and phases of the believer's life.

The Apostle Paul identifies these three *distinct* dimensions ***as spirit, and soul and body,*** having in view the *sanctification and preservation of the entire being of man.* This is what is meant by being ***"sanctified wholly."*** The Bible clearly teaches that man is a *tri-partite* being and *exists in three dimensions or spheres.* Genesis records:

And the LORD God formed man of the dust of the ground [**body**], *and breathed into his nostrils the breath of life* [**spirit**]; *and man became a living* **soul.**

(Gen. 2:7, emphasis added)

When Adam sinned, the process of death began to work in him.

: for in the day that thou eatest thereof thou shalt surely die.

(Gen 2:17)

Death affected Adam in all three dimensions of his being—*spirit, soul, and body.* However, *death did not occur in each dimension at the same time.*

Adam died instantly in his spirit and progressively in his soul and body. Although ***the process of physical death*** *began the day he ate from the forbidden tree, physically Adam lived for hundreds of years before physical death claimed him* (Gen. 5:5; 2 Pet. 3:8). However, *spiritual death claimed him immediately* just as God promised (Gen. 2:17).

Adam died within his *spirit* and *soul* as he experienced *separation from God, guilt, condemnation, and fear.* When *Adam received the blood atonement by faith,* Adam was redeemed. Adam again found favor with God, and *his fellowship with God was restored.* Adam was *then sanctified* (made holy in spirit, soul, and body) *on the basis of that atonement* and became the first ***heir*** to *the righteousness which is by faith* (Heb. 11:7). Likewise:

When a man or woman by faith receives Jesus Christ as Savior, regeneration and sanctification occur instantly in man's spirit.

Notice *Paul, speaking by the Holy Ghost, reveals the process of sanctification and preservation in the precise order* of ***spirit, soul, and body***. This is no coincidence. Why is this significant? When we consider the doctrine *"we are saved to be saved,"* we should have in mind the following picture.

The redemption of **the whole man** *occurs in three dimensions, phases, or spheres.* ***Redemption of the spirit, redemption of the soul, and redemption of the body*** (1 Thess. 5:23).

<u>*Redemption of the Whole Man*</u>

- ***<u>The spirit</u>*** *of man is redeemed and* ***instantly regenerated*** *at the moment one receives Christ and the inward man is renewed day by day* (2 Cor. 4:16).

- ***<u>The soul</u>*** *of man* (mind, emotions, and will) *is redeemed and is* ***progressively being transformed*** *from the influence* *and control of the flesh or carnal nature to the influence and control of the Spirit. It is this part of man that must be crucified daily along with the carnal mind and fleshly desires that war in our members* (Rom. 12:2; Gal. 5:24).

- ***<u>The body</u>*** *of the outward man* ***continues to perish daily through aging*** *and will be* ***redeemed or translated*** *into a glorified body at the coming of the Lord* (2 Cor. 4:16; Rom. 8:23; 1 Cor. 15:51-54; 1 Thess. 4:16-17).

In our dimension of *time and space*, man is *born again* or regenerated in the sequence of *spirit, soul, and body*. The believer is *wholly saved* and *sanctified instantly.* The moment he receives Christ, he is at that moment a new creature (creation) in Christ (2 Cor. 5:17).

Yet, at the same time, ***his soul is progressively transformed into the image of Christ*** *by the renewing of his mind; as his carnal nature* (the old man which is yet present) *is daily brought under subjection to the nature of Christ* (the new man that now dwells within him) (Rom. 8:29,12:2; Tit. 3:5; 2 Cor. 4:16; Eph. 4:23-24). This *phase* or dimension of salvation continues throughout the believer's natural life and is *the work of the Holy Spirit* through what we shall refer to as *"sanctifying grace."*

The final phase of the believer's salvation includes the redemption of his body (Rom. 8:23), at which time his physical body will be *born again, translated, or changed* at the coming of the Lord (1 Cor. 15:51). This is what Paul calls ***the blessed hope*** of the believer (Tit. 2:13).

It is important to understand that all of these *redemptive processes* occur (in our reality) in *the dimension of time and space* at some point during the believer's lifetime. However, in God's dimension of *eternity*, these redemptive processes have ***already*** been accomplished and finished in Christ.

It is within this context that each dimension or part of man (spirit, soul, and body) is *sanctified* and ***kept by the power of God through faith*** in a state of *preservation unto the day of Jesus Christ* (1 Pet. 1:5). In the matter of the believer's salvation and his eternal security, we have the promise and the assurance of God's Word.

Being confident of this very thing, that he which hath begun a

good work in you will perform it until the day of Jesus Christ:
(Phil. 1:6)

It is within this context that the believer is exhorted "to work out your own salvation with fear and trembling" (Phil. 2:12). ***This does not mean that the believer is responsible to save himself through works, or that he will be eternally lost if he fails to perform the work of sanctification himself.*** This means that:

The believer is responsible only to allow the Holy Spirit by faith to do the work of salvation and sanctification within him by yielding to the transforming and renewing work of the Holy Spirit. In other words, the believer will "conform" as the "Spirit" transforms" (Rom. 6:13-19, 12:1-2).

Lest the believer should think within himself that he is responsible for this saving and sanctifying work of God's grace, the Apostle Paul continues later by saying,

For it is God which worketh in you both to will and to do of his good pleasure.
(Phil. 2:13)

In summary, holiness is not the work of the believer. *Sanctification and preservation are both the work of the Holy Spirit.* However, it is the believer's responsibility to *yield the right of way* and *submit his free will* to *the will of the Holy Spirit.* As we yield ourselves to the Holy Spirit, He *worketh* in us, or performs the work of sanctification in our lives. As the believer yields himself to the sanctifying agency of *the spirit of holiness* and the *Word of God*, He makes us holy through *the blood and Spirit of Jesus Christ.*

Preservation is possible only because it is based on the ***finished*** *work of Christ.* The writer to the Hebrews *ties the perfection and sanctification of the believer to the substitution and atonement of Christ at Calvary.* Writing by the Spirit, he says:

For by one offering he hath perfected for ever them that are sanctified.
(Heb. 10:14)

Sinless Perfection?

If we say that we have no sin, we deceive ourselves, and the truth is not in us.

(1 Jn. 1:8)

The concept of *sinless perfection* or *living without committing sin* is a lofty ideal but is neither practical nor possible as long as we are in *the flesh*. The Bible is clear. As mortals, we have *a sinful nature* and *everyone* this side of heaven commits sin *every day*. There are no exceptions—no one is excluded.

No, we are not all drunkards, adulterers, and murderers, but *we are all sinners by nature* and unfortunately, we do commit sins of *commission* and *omission* every day. Even those who are proud and preach the loudest against sin saying, *"you don't have to sin a little bit every day"* commit sin in some form every day.

Recently, I sat under the ministry of a well-known television evangelist. I was truly blessed by his ministry, especially his insight into stewardship and giving. However, I recoiled with shock as he boasted of how he did not sin every day, and that he could go days without sinning.

I don't know what kind of sin he had in mind, but I do know better than to make such a statement. I believe this is poor theology, especially when the Bible says, "the thought of foolishness is sin" (Prov. 24:9).

As we have mentioned before, *spiritual pride is the mother of all sin.* It is iniquity of the worst kind, because *it blinds us to our own corruption. Spiritual pride breeds self-righteousness and boasting.* Remember, one does not have to commit an *overt* act in order to be guilty of sin in his heart. Jesus said:

But I say unto you, That whosoever looketh on a woman to lust after her hath committed adultery with her already in his heart.

(Matt. 5:28)

Jesus taught us that *sin originates in the heart*, even if it is not expressed or seen openly. Even though we have a *new nature*, which is of God (which cannot sin), we still have the *old nature* of sin (which does sin). This nature is a part of us until we are translated to be with Jesus.

For there is not a just man upon earth, that doeth good, and sinneth not.

(Eccl. 7:20)

"*The preacher*" *is not* saying that there is not a just man upon the earth, for we know there are many just men on the earth. He is simply saying that even though there are just men upon the earth who do good, yet they are also at the same time found to be sinners in need of God's mercy and grace. The Apostle John said,

If we say that we have no sin, we deceive ourselves, and the truth is not in us.

(1 Jn. 1:8)

Christ Jesus, due to his *virgin* birth, was the *only person ever born without a sin nature.* **He did not sin** at all—at any time in his entire life (1 Pet. 2:22). Other than Jesus Christ, the perfect man,

...all have sinned and come short of the glory of God.
(Rom. 3:23)

Jesus Christ is the only sinless and perfect man.

This does not take away from the teaching of living ***a victorious life****, a* ***Spirit filled*** *and* ***Spirit controlled life.*** The *thought life* and the *motivations of the heart—pride, envy, lust, unforgiveness, etc.—will* frequently challenge *all* Christians and must be confronted and confessed as they arise. The important thing is:

The Bible does not teach that we will not struggle with sin as believers. The Bible teaches that because we are now in Christ, we are not to allow our sin nature to rule, reign, or have dominion over us (Rom. 6:14).

Sinless perfection therefore cannot be achieved in this dimension of *flesh and blood,* except to say that,

In the same manner that we are holy in Christ, we are also found in Christ to be sinless and perfect in the sight of God the Father through the shed blood of Jesus Christ.

So, why then are believers exhorted to live holy and to live separate from sin?

Believers are exhorted to live Christ-like for two reasons

1) Because Christ is holy

2) To be an effective witness for Christ

With enough having been said about sanctification, let us look at the aspect of preservation a little closer.

The Spirit, the Water, and the Blood

And there are three that bear witness in earth, the spirit, and the water, and the blood: and these three agree in one.

(1 Jn. 5:8)

But one of the soldiers with a spear pierced his side, and forthwith came there out blood and water.

(Jn. 19:34)

Jude, the servant of Jesus Christ, and brother of James, to them that are sanctified by God the Father, and preserved in Jesus Christ, and called:

(Jude 1)

One of the most compelling scriptures to support the doctrine of the preservation of the believer is found in Paul's letter to the Ephesians.

> *And grieve not the holy Spirit of God, whereby ye are sealed unto the day of redemption.*
>
> (Eph. 4:30, emphasis added)

In this scripture, the Greek word used here for ***sealed*** is *sphragis*. It literally means ***to stamp for security or preservation***. In the matter of the security of the believer, *to be preserved is to be* ***sealed unto eternal life****. It is to* ***keep*** *or* ***protect from perishing.***

My mind goes back to the time when I was a young child. In my neighborhood, folks used to *can fruit and other foodstuffs* in glass jars called *Mason jars*. These foodstuffs were called ***preserves***. (I can still see them in my mind, lined up in a row on a basement shelf). It involved a canning *process* in which food was *cleansed*, placed in the jars and heated in *water* to a temperature high enough to kill the bacteria and other microorganisms.

As the jar cools, air is forced from the jar and a vacuum is created. The jar is then hermetically ***sealed*** with a special self-sealing rubber lid, which prevents air from re-entering the jar, bringing with it bacteria and other contaminating organisms. Food prepared in this manner was *preserved* without contamination and could be stored for months or perhaps years until the day it was ready to be eaten. What an illustration. In like manner,

> ***God is not only able to save the believer, but He is able to keep the believer in a state of preservation because he is sealed unto the day of redemption*** (Eph. 4:30).

I believe that just as food is *cleansed, sealed, and preserved, in a spiritual sense:*

> ***The Spirit, the water, and the blood work together in the salvation and preservation of the believer. These witness or testify to the finished work of Calvary. The believer in Jesus Christ is cleansed, sealed and preserved blameless unto the coming of our Lord Jesus Christ*** (1 Thess. 5:23).

- ***<u>The Spirit</u>*** *bears witness that we are* **sealed.**

- ***<u>The water</u>*** *bears witness that we are* ***cleansed.***

- ***<u>The blood</u>*** *bears witness that we are* ***preserved.***

Notice *the believer is not only preserved, but he is preserved* ***blameless***. Jude begins his epistle by stating that the believer in Christ is *sanctified by God the Father* and ***preserved in Christ Jesus.***

To ***preserve*** *(Gr. teresis)* is to: *guard (from loss or injury) by keeping the eye upon, to hold fast, preserve, keep watch.*

To be preserved *blameless* means—*to be preserved* ***without fault, spot, or blemish***. Jude ends his epistle by declaring that *God our Savior* is *able* ***to keep you from falling****, and to present you* ***faultless*** *before the presence of his glory with exceeding joy* (Jude 24).

The believer is not preserved blameless on the basis of *his* works. He is preserved blameless on the basis of *his faith* in the finished work of Christ at Calvary (1 Pet. 1:5).

Son-ship vs. Servant-hood

Every man's work shall be made manifest: for the day shall declare it, because it shall be revealed by fire; and the fire shall try every man's work of what sort it is. If any man's work abide which he hath built thereupon, he shall receive a reward. If any man's work shall be burned, he shall suffer loss: but he himself shall be saved; yet so as by fire.

(1 Cor. 3:13-15)

Paul, a servant of Jesus Christ, called to be an apostle, separated unto the gospel of God,

(Rom.1:1)

One of the reasons why the legalist places an emphasis on works to be saved is because he has a contextual misunderstanding of the use of the term ***reward*** as it relates to his salvation and heaven. Likewise,

The use of the term "reward" will appear awkward to the believer who does not understand the basis for which he is saved and the basis upon which rewards are given in heaven.

The lingering question for some is:

If salvation and righteousness is *a free gift,* ***then on what basis is the believer promised rewards and crowns when he gets to heaven and stands before the judgment seat of Christ*** (Rom. 5:15-18)? ***How can it be said that the believer is*** *saved by grace without works,* ***if at the same time he is to*** *run or work* ***in order that he may obtain a crown of reward in heaven*** (1 Cor. 9:24)?

I believe the Holy Spirit has given the church some understanding in this area. It is not very hard to understand when one considers the following.

Much of the confusion surrounding the receiving of rewards in heaven centers on misunderstanding the two aspects *of our relationship to God the Father and our Lord Jesus Christ* (Rom. 1:7). These are the aspects of *Son-ship and Servant-hood.*

- ***<u>God the Father</u>***: *A believer is a* ***son of God and an heir*** *through the* ***adoption of the New Birth*** (Eph. 1:5).
- ***<u>The Lord Jesus Christ</u>***: *A believer is then called to be* ***a servant*** (or bond slave) *through the* ***Lordship*** *of Jesus Christ* (Rom. 1:1; Jude 1:1).

You see, a believer is both ***a son*** *of God the Father and* ***a servant*** *of Jesus Christ.* As grace believers, we must understand that ***man cannot earn salvation. It is a free gift.*** More importantly, ***if one cannot earn it through human merit, one cannot maintain it through human merit.*** A believer can, however, *lay up treasure* or rewards *in heaven a*fter being saved. However,

The believer's reward or treasure in heaven is based on his life's work of service which he has built upon the foundation of

the finished work of Christ, as a servant or steward of God and not based on his adoption as a son (Matt. 6:19; 1 Cor. 3:11-12).

The ***judgment (bema) seat of Christ is the judgment of the believer's works.*** This will take place *in heaven* ***after*** the *rapture* of the church and prior to His Second Coming. Jesus Christ our Lord will call his servants (*the church triumphant*) and give to them *crowns* and *rewards* based on their ***work*** *of service to Christ.* However, as *sons of God the Father,* we are **heirs to the kingdom, and shall inherit all things** by **birthright** (Rom. 14:10; 1 Cor. 3:13-15, Rev. 21:7).

The judgment seat of Christ is the *final* judgment for the believer.

The believer's sins will not be judged here.

Why? The believer's sins *were already judged* in Christ at Calvary. They are not at issue here. The believer should have no fear that his sin will follow him to the *Bema* judgement, because through the blood of Jesus *his sins have gone before him to judgment* (1 Tim. 5:24).

When the believer stands before God, it will be to give an *account for his service.* It is not to give an account for his sin. Only the believer's *works* and *motives* as a servant will be judged at the *Bema seat.* In fact, the Word of God promises:

As far as the east is from the west, so far hath he removed our transgressions from us.

(Psa. 103:12)

...for thou hast cast all my sins behind thy back.

(Isa. 38:17)

And their sins and iniquities will I remember no more.

(Heb. 10:17)

In the matter of the eternal security of the believer, I am a *son* and a *servant*. As a servant, I may *suffer loss* at *the judgment seat of*

Christ. My work for Jesus as a servant may not survive the test of *fire* and be *burned* up. I may lose some or all of my reward. However, ***I will not lose my salvation.***

Though I may have *gone astray* and have *grieved the Holy Spirit* at times in my life and *not walked in victory;* though my *poor quality of service* (wood, hay, and stubble) may be burned up, *I am still* ***sealed unto*** (not until) ***the day of redemption*** (Eph. 4:30). ***I shall be saved yet so as by fire*** (1 Cor. 3:13-15).

In conclusion, I am ***a son***, *saved by grace through faith in the shed blood of Jesus Christ.* At the same time, I am ***a servant*** (or steward), serving Christ according to the talents or the ability that He gives me.

Heaven is an *inheritance* because of *son-ship.* We are *heirs* to the kingdom; we are given a reward on the basis of *servant-hood.* As grace believers, we don't work to get to heaven, but *we do work as servants* of Christ and will receive *rewards of inheritance* when we get there (Rev. 21:7). Paul says this ***reward is reckoned of grace*** (Rom. 4:4,16).

New Testament believers will not always be servants. In the age to come others will serve and we will be *kings and priests unto our God* (Rev. 1:6). We will always be sons.

Reprobation:

That process
whereby those who were once enlightened,
and

having had saving knowledge of Jesus Christ
and profession of the same,

Who, through continual resisting of the Holy Ghost
in unbelief and hardness of the heart,
and

having done despite to the Spirit of grace,
are then given over to a final and lasting state of
apostasy,
and

are disqualified of eternal life, having fallen away from
enduring faith in the blood atonement,
and

do deny the work of the Holy Ghost
wrought through
the finished work of Jesus Christ at Calvary.

16

Reprobation

When we introduced the subject of the eternal security of the believer, the question was raised:

Can a believer ever lose his salvation and be eternally lost?

Perhaps you are one who sincerely believes that a believer can be lost after he is saved. Perhaps you are not. Perhaps you skipped ahead in this book just to get to this subject. Well, I am not going to disappoint you. We are going to expend some effort here and visit a very controversial subject. That is, *the doctrine of reprobation.*

Nothing I have dealt with thus far has given me more pause and prayerfulness than dealing with the question of the eternal security of the believer. What I believe about what the Bible teaches in this regard is not important. What is important is *what you believe about eternal security and the assurance of your own salvation.*

Because of the difficulty and variety of opinions surrounding the doctrine of *reprobation*, I would just rather leave this subject out of this work altogether. However, God will not let me. I know that I may lose some of you who have been with me up to now. Some, who have not been on board may indeed come on board at this juncture. We will not agree on all points of doctrine. Nevertheless, we cannot evade our responsibility to deal with any doctrine simply because it may be highly controversial or difficult to understand or communicate. I will therefore declare my position from the outset. That is,

Your works of righteousness have nothing whatsoever to do with your eternal security; however, your enduring faith in the blood atonement of Jesus Christ does.

We know that a believer may *backslide* at times during his life. We also know that a believer may also slip into *heresy* and embrace *false doctrine* (teaching) that will *pervert* the gospel of Jesus Christ and distort his understanding of the truth (Gal. 1:6). However,

How does one move from backsliding to becoming reprobate?

The Three Phases of Apostasy

Just as sanctification is a *process* and occurs in *three dimensions and phases* of the believer's life, it is my belief that:

Apostasy (falling away) ***is a process of spiritual decline and can occur in three dimensions and phases of the believer's life.***

There are Three Phases of Apostasy:

1) *The* **Prodigal phase** *of drawing back*
2) *The* **Apostate phase** *of falling away*
3) *The* **Reprobate phase** *of no return*

I say apostasy is *a process* that *can* occur, because one *does not* have to experience any phase of apostasy at all, or one may experience *one, two, or all three phases of apostasy.* Each *phase* represents *a dimension and a degree* to which one has *fallen away* and denotes the *seriousness* of one's condition of spiritual decline. *Phases one and two* are *transitional states of being* that can be experienced in any order, depending on *the reasons or circumstances which* brought about the *backsliding* or *apostasy* in the first place (i.e. rebellion, heresy, etc.).

- In *phase one—the* prodigal *does not* change his *belief system.* He believes the truth, however *he does not walk in faith. He walks according to the flesh and in disobedience.*

- In *phase two—an* apostate on the other hand actually *changes his belief system*, embraces *another gospel*, and perverts the gospel of Christ (Gal. 1:6-7). He may depart from *the faith* but not necessarily withdraw from fellowship.

There are Three Dimensions of Apostasy:

*1) The dimension of the **mind.***
*2) The dimension of the **will.***
*3) The dimension of the **emotions.***

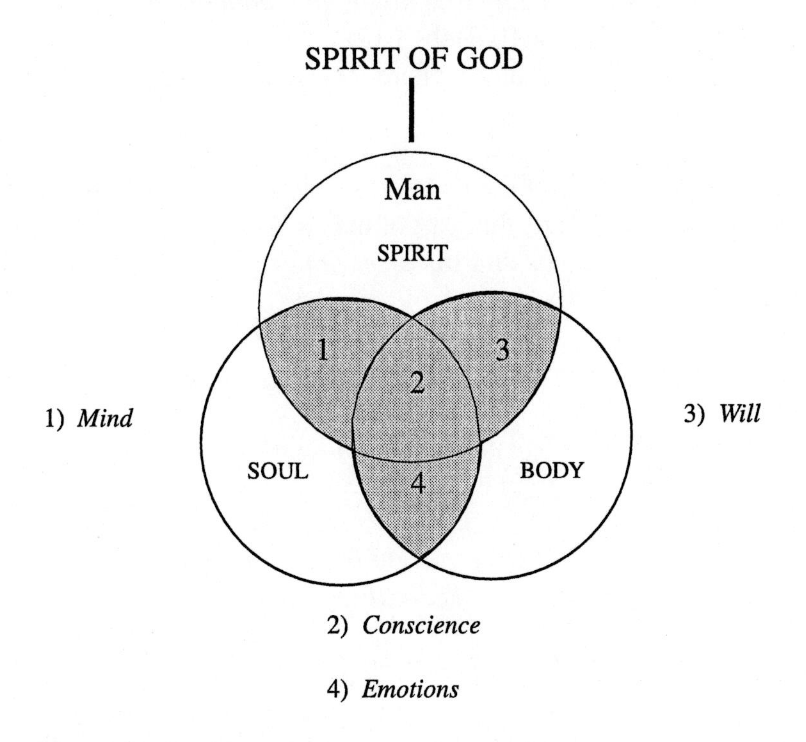

Apostasy begins in the heart. Why the heart? Because:

- The heart is *the control center of the soul* (mind, will, and emotions).
- The heart is *the interface or connecting point* between the

soul and spirit (Heb. 4:12).

- The heart is the *link* to *the spirit of man* that links him to *the Spirit of God.*
- The heart is where *spiritual understanding* takes place (Matt. 13:15).
- The heart is the place from whence proceed *the issues of life* (Prov. 4:23).
- The heart is the place where *sin* originates (Matt. 15:18-19).
- The heart *directs the thought life of the mind.* For "as he thinketh in his heart so is he:" (Prov. 23:7).
- The heart is where *faith, doubt, and unbelief reside* (Mk. 11:23, Rom.10: 10, Heb. 3:12).
- The heart is the place where *love, apathy, or rejection of God* begins.

As apostasy affects a man's heart, it also affects his *mind* and *will.* Apostasy also affects that part of man's *soul and spirit* wherein dwells man's *conscience* and his *discernment of right and wrong* (Heb. 10:22; 1 Jn. 3:20).

When a man's conscience is affected by apostasy

- *His ability to feel conviction and guilt for sin and to discern right from wrong is also affected.*

- *His inability to discern right from wrong then affects his volition or will and his ability to choose right from wrong.*

When one continues *unrepentant* in this *phase* or *final state of apostasy,* there comes a time when, as *potter's clay,* one becomes *hardened in his heart.* He no longer *feels or responds* to the *reproof or conviction* of *sin, righteousness, and judgment* that the Holy Spirit ministers to him (Jn. 16:8; Rom. 2:5). This is the *critical or reprobate phase of apostasy* for which there is no remedy and from which there is no return.

As we examine *the three phases of apostasy,* a word needs to be said about backsliding in general.

- *We must remember that there is a definite* ***spiritual distinction*** *between a prodigal, an apostate, and a reprobate.*

- *We must remember that God has* ***a redemptive relationship covenant*** *with the backslider* (Jer. 3:14).

- *We must remember that God sees backsliding as a debilitating spiritual condition which requires* ***healing.***

For God declares in Jeremiah,

Turn*, O backsliding children, saith the LORD; for I am* ***married*** *unto you:...*
(Jer. 3:14)

Return*, ye backsliding children, and I will* ***heal*** *your backslidings...*
(Jer. 3:22)

These scriptures reveal that God *loves* the backslider, is in a *covenant relationship* with him and promises to *heal, cure, or mend* the backslider's condition of spiritual decline, if the backslider will ***turn*** from his ways and ***return*** to the Lord.

The Prodigal Phase

And he said, A certain man had two sons: And the younger of them said to his father, Father, give me the portion of goods that falleth to me. And he divided unto them his living. And not many days after the younger son gathered all together, and took his journey into a far country, and there wasted his substance with riotous living. And when he had spent all, there arose a mighty famine in that land; and he began to be in want. And he went and joined himself to a citizen of that country; and he sent him into his fields to feed swine. And he would fain have filled his belly with the husks that the swine did eat: and no man gave unto him. And when he came to himself, he said, How many hired servants of my father's have bread enough and to spare, and I perish with hunger! I will arise and go to my father, and will say unto him, Father, I have sinned against heaven, and before thee, And am no more worthy to be called thy son: make me as one of thy hired servants. And he arose, and came to his father. But when he was yet a great way off, his father saw him, and had compassion, and ran, and fell on his neck, and kissed him. And the son said unto him, Father, I have sinned against heaven, and in thy sight, and am no more worthy to be called thy son. But the father said to his servants, Bring forth the best robe, and put it on him; and put a ring on his hand, and shoes on his feet: And bring hither the fatted calf, and kill it; and let us eat, and be merry: For this my son was dead, and is alive again; he was lost, and is found. And they began to be merry. Now his elder son was in the field: and as he came and drew nigh to the house, he heard musick and dancing. And he called one of the servants, and asked what these things meant. And he said unto him, Thy brother is come; and thy father hath killed the fatted calf, because he hath received him safe and sound. And he was angry, and would not go in: therefore came his father out, and intreated him. And he answering said to his father, Lo, these many years do I serve thee, neither transgressed I at any time thy commandment: and yet thou never gavest me a kid, that I might make merry with my friends: But as soon as this thy son was come, which hath devoured thy living with harlots, thou hast killed for him the fatted calf. And he said unto him, Son, thou art ever with me, and all that I have is thine. It was meet that we should make merry, and be glad: for this thy brother was dead, and is alive again; and was lost, and is found.

(Lk. 15: 11-32)

Drawing Back

What does it mean to backslide? *To backslide is to* ***draw back*** *from the worship, service, and fellowship of God* (Heb. 10:38). Backsliding usually occurs in *the first phase of apostasy.* It is the wasteful or ***prodigal phase,*** when a believer may *leave or forsake:*

- *The Father's* ***table***
- *The Father's* ***fellowship***
- *The Father's* ***house***

However, there is one characteristic difference between the backsliding prodigal and the apostate. *Unlike the apostate, the prodigal does not forsake his father's faith.* **He still believes in the gospel of Jesus Christ and the blood atonement.** *An important point needs to be made here:*

In the first two phases of apostasy, a backslider's heart can still be dealt with by the Holy Spirit and repentance and restoration is still possible. However, in the final phase of apostasy, repentance and restoration are not possible due to unbelief and hardness of heart (Heb. 6:4).

The *prodigal phase* is the phase most commonly experienced in the church, but it is far from the *final* (or reprobate) *phase* of apostasy. In fact, ***the believer may not leave the father's house at all but may be backslid in his heart.*** The book of Proverbs says:

The backslider in heart shall be filled with his own ways:...
(Prov. 14:14)

<u>*There are Definite Signs of Backsliding:*</u>

1) A decrease in Christ centered worship evidenced by a lack of church attendance, prayer, praise, and giving.

2) An increase in the level of discontent evidenced by murmuring and complaining, an attitude of ingratitude, willful disobedience, and unwilling service to the Father.

<u>*People Turn Their Backs on God for Any Number of Reasons:*</u>

- *Some are* **tempted**, *fall into sin, and do not soon repent.*

- *Some are* **angry** *with God because of some situation or* *circumstance in their life gone awry.*

- *Some are* **bitter,** *rebellious, and stubborn against God's will for their lives.*

- *Some have been* **hurt** *by the church membership or leadership.*

One may backslide and *withdraw* from fellowship for any combination of the above. ***This does not mean, however, that they will be lost or lose their salvation.*** It simply means they have embarked on a *spiritual journey* away from God's *perfect will.* They will enter God's *permissive will* and it will ultimately bring them back to God and to His perfect will for their lives.

This *journey of disobedience* will be played out in circumstances that will permit the *chastisement* (discipline) *and correction of God* (Heb. 12:6-13). This discipline will ultimately *correct* or *make straight* their path, and they will find themselves again in the presence of a Father who is waiting with open arms to receive them because they are ***sons***—they are his children.

The parable of *The Prodigal Son* reveals the heart of God toward the backslider. It is one of *love, compassion, mercy, and great longsuffering.* I would encourage all believers to study carefully the wonderful message of God's *redemptive grace* portrayed in this parable. Notice the attitude of each son, but especially the attitude of the Father toward them both.

This parable teaches us about the two aspects of *relationship* and *fellowship.* These are often misunderstood in the case of the backslider. In order to understand how God's *sovereign grace* works in the life of the backslider, we must understand that *there is a difference between the two.* One aspect is subject to change. One is not.

What is the Difference Between Relationship and Fellowship?

- ***Relationship*:** has to do with our *standing* or *position in Christ.* The aspect of relationship *is not* subject to change. Regardless of the *fruitfulness, level of maturity,* *or degree of victory* in the believer's life, we are adopted *sons and daughters, heirs of God, and joint heirs* with Christ.

- ***Fellowship*:** has to do with the *quality* or *level of intimacy* of our relationship with Christ. *It can range from intimacy and complete submission, to estrangement and rebellion.* The aspect of fellowship is *subject to change* and directly affects the *fruitfulness, level of maturity, and the degree of victory* in the believer's life.

How does sin affect the believer in the aspects of relationship and fellowship?

The answer is really quite simple. *Sin* (disobedience) *separates the believer from intimate fellowship with the Father, but sin cannot separate us from His love, favor, and our standing as sons and daughters.*

As a son, regardless of the quality of our fellowship or lack thereof, our relationship to God the Father remains the same.

We are still sons and daughters of God, though we, like the prodigal, may at times be *disobedient* and go our own way. It is my belief that though a son may stray from *the household of faith,* ***as long as his faith remains in the shed blood of Jesus and the finished work of Calvary,*** he will in due time return to *the household of faith* as did the prodigal. What all believers must understand is:

All of the believer's sins (past, present, and future) ***have been paid for in full by the blood of Jesus.***

Furthermore, because the believer appropriates God's forgiveness through *enduring faith* in the blood of Jesus and the finished work of Calvary:

Sin may indeed separate the believer from fellowship, but it cannot separate the believer from relationship or eternal life.

This is hard for the legalist to accept, because his standing with God is based on human merit rather than the merit of the shed blood of Jesus Christ.

What about Christians who fall into a lifestyle of sin?

The Bible says, "A righteous man falling down before the wicked is as a troubled fountain, and a corrupt spring" (Prov. 25:26).

Any Christian who falls before unbelievers brings shame to the *Body of Christ*, causes those who are not saved to blaspheme and causes those in the faith to stumble. However, the Bible also says:

For a just man falleth seven times, and riseth up again:...
(Prov. 24:16)

The apostle John writes:

Whosoever is born of God doth not commit sin; for his seed remaineth in him: and he cannot sin, because he is born of God.
(1 Jn: 3:9)

This verse is interpreted to mean that he that is born of God does not ***"practice"*** *sin because God's* seed *or* nature *remains in him. Eventually the* Holy Spirit *will bring the erring believer back into fellowship with God or will take the believer home prematurely through the chastisement of God* (Acts 5:1-11; 1 Cor. 5:1-5, 11:28-32).

Those prodigals that fall away from *faith* or depart from fellowship, indeed may be *unfruitful, lack spiritual maturity, and have no victory over the flesh, the world, and the devil.* However, ***they are still saved as long as they possess enduring faith in the blood of Jesus Christ.*** On the other hand, those prodigals who *depart from* ***"the faith"*** or from *the doctrine of the blood atonement of Jesus Christ* are of the ***apostasia*** *(Gk.)* or *the falling away*. These have *gone in the way of Cain* and have entered the *second phase* of Apostasy (Jude 11).

The Apostate Phase

Now the Spirit speaketh expressly, that in the latter times ***some shall depart from the faith,*** *giving heed to seducing spirits, and doctrines of devils; Speaking lies in hypocrisy;* ***having their conscience seared*** *with a hot iron;*

(1 Tim. 4:1-2, emphasis added)

But there were false prophets also among the people, even as there shall be false teachers among you, who privily shall bring in ***damnable heresies,*** *even* ***denying the Lord that bought them,*** *and bring upon themselves swift destruction. And many shall follow their pernicious ways; by reason of whom the way of truth shall be evil spoken of.*

(2 Pet. 2:1-2, emphasis added)

Beloved, when I gave all diligence to write unto you of the common salvation, it was needful for me to write unto you, and exhort you that ye should earnestly contend for ***the faith*** *which was once delivered unto the saints. For there are certain men crept in unawares, who were before of old ordained to this condemnation, ungodly men, turning the grace of our God into lasciviousness, and* ***denying the only Lord God, and our Lord Jesus Christ.***

(Jude 3-4, emphasis added)

Falling Away

An *apostate* is one who *falls away* from ***the truth*** and ***departs from the faith.*** *An apostate who is also a teacher is a heretic and usually embraces false doctrine which is central to the theme of salvation, such as:*

- *denying or rejecting the* ***virgin birth,***
- *denying or rejecting the* ***deity of Christ***
- *denying or rejecting the* ***blood atonement, or***
- *denying or rejecting the* ***work of the Holy Spirit, etc.***

Earlier, I made the assertion that *Cain was the first apostate referenced* in scripture. Why? Because:

Cain fell away or departed from the faith delivered to him by his father.

By embracing *the false religion of* **righteousness through works** (legalism), *Cain fell away or departed from the principle of faith in the blood atonement.* You see,

In order for one to qualify as an apostate, one must first have walked in the light of truth and then abandoned the truth to embrace error.

The Acts of the Apostates

But chiefly them that ***walk after the flesh*** *in the lust of uncleanness, and* ***despise government. Presumptuous*** *are they,* ***selfwilled,*** *they* ***are not afraid to speak evil*** *of dignities... But these, as* ***natural brute beasts****, made to be taken and destroyed,* ***speak evil of the things that they understand not;*** *and shall utterly perish in their own corruption; And shall receive the reward of unrighteousness, as they that count it pleasure to riot in the day time. Spots they are and blemishes, sporting themselves with their own deceivings while they feast with you; Having eyes full of adultery, and that cannot cease from sin; beguiling unstable souls: an heart they have exercised with covetous practices; cursed children:* ***Which have forsaken the right way, and are gone astray****, following the way of Balaam the son of Bosor, who loved the wages of unrighteousness;... These are* ***wells without water, clouds that are carried with a tempest:*** *to whom the mist of darkness is reserved for ever. For when they speak great swelling words of vanity, they allure through the lusts of the flesh, through much wantonness, those that were clean escaped from them who live in error. While they promise them liberty, they themselves are the* ***servants of corruption****: for of whom a man is overcome, of the same is he brought in bondage.* ***For if after they have escaped the pollutions of the world through the knowledge of the Lord and Saviour Jesus Christ, they are again entangled therein, and overcome, the latter end is worse with***

them than the beginning. For it had been better for them not to have known the way of righteousness, than, after they have known it, to turn from the holy commandment delivered unto them. *But it is happened unto them according to the true proverb, The dog is turned to his own vomit again; and the sow that was washed to her wallowing in the mire.*

(2 Pet. 2:10, 12-15, 17-22, emphasis added)

In warning about *the acts of the apostate,* the apostle Peter and Jude, our Lord's brother, refer to these as *false teachers, filthy dreamers, brute beasts,* and those who have ***gone in the way of Cain*** (Jude 11). These are they who embrace and *bring in* ***damnable heresies, even denying the Lord who bought them*** (2 Pet. 2:1). In other words, in the *spirit* of Cain, ***they deny the finished work of Christ as their redeemer*** (Jude 1:4). They are *heretics (false teachers)* of the worst sort. Not only do these apostates *deny the blood atonement of Jesus Christ*, they live *ungodly*, and consequently teach others to do the same. Of these it is written,

Likewise also these filthy dreamers defile the flesh, ***despise dominion,*** *and speak evil of dignities. Yet Michael the archangel, when contending with the devil he disputed about the body of Moses, durst not bring against him a railing accusation, but said, The Lord rebuke thee. But these speak evil of those things which they know not: but what they know naturally, as* ***brute beasts****, in those things they corrupt themselves.* ***Woe unto them! for they have gone in the way of Cain,*** *and ran greedily after the error of Balaam for reward, and perished in the gainsaying of Core. These are* ***spots in your feasts of charity,*** *when they feast with you, feeding themselves without fear:* ***clouds they are without water****, carried about of winds;* ***trees whose fruit withereth,*** *without fruit, twice dead, plucked up by the roots;* ***Raging waves of the sea,*** *foaming out their own shame;* ***wandering stars****, to whom is reserved the blackness of darkness for ever... These are* ***murmurers, complainers,*** *walking after their own lusts; and their mouth speaketh great swelling words, having men's persons in admiration because of advantage. But, beloved, remember ye the words which were spoken before of the apostles of our Lord Jesus Christ; How that they told you there* *should be mockers in the last time, who should walk after their own ungodly lusts. These be they who separate themselves,* ***sensual, having not the Spirit.***

(Jude 8-13, 16-19, emphasis added)

It is evident from the writings of Peter and Jude that the sanctifying agencies of the Holy Spirit can no longer be seen in the life of the apostate, as they are now called ***natural brute beasts***, and are said to be ***sensual*** and ***having not the Spirit.*** Could this perhaps suggest that these are not truly born of ***the Spirit of Christ*** at all and therefore are in actuality ***none of His*** (Rom. 8:9)?

Some would suggest that the scriptures in the book of Hebrews and others which speak of ***falling away*** *indicate that the apostate may not be genuinely saved at all,* since he has only *a limited experience* with the means of grace. He has only ***tasted*** *the heavenly gift, the Word of God, and the powers of the world to come.* Yet, he is said to have ***been made a partaker of the Holy Ghost.*** Further yet, they are said to *have* ***fallen*** *to a place from whence they cannot be restored.*

How can this be? *How can one depart from the faith if he was never in the faith to begin with?* It is my opinion that these scriptures refer to those apostates who have entered the final phase of apostasy.

The Reprobate Phase

Now as Jannes and Jambres withstood Moses, so do these also resist the truth: men of corrupt minds, **reprobate** *concerning* ***the faith.***

(2 Tim. 3:8, emphasis added)

Examine yourselves*, whether ye be in* ***the faith; prove your own selves.*** *Know ye not your own selves, how that Jesus Christ is in you, except ye be reprobates?*

(2 Cor. 13:5, emphasis added)

The final phase of apostasy is that of the *reprobate.* Some may be wondering, ***What is a reprobate?***

A reprobate is one who has entered the critical phase of apostasy and has passed the point from which he can no longer return.

The word *reprobate* comes from the Greek word *adokimos*, which translated means *disapproved and rejected. A reprobate is one whom after being examined* **is not found to be a genuine believer**. *He has* ***failed the test*** *of enduring saving faith, is* ***disqualified, disapproved,*** *and* ***rejected*** *as* **counterfeit.**

> *The Apostle Paul admonished the Corinthians to do two things.*
>
> *1) Examine* themselves, and to *prove or test* themselves to ensure they were in ***the faith.***
>
> *2) Examine* themselves, and *know how* that Jesus Christ (in truth) dwelt within them.

They were to do this to assure themselves that they were *genuine* believers and not counterfeit or *reprobate.* Although it may be difficult for some of us to accept the truth that there are those among us who are *not all of us* (1 Jn. 2:19),

There is simply too much scriptural evidence to dismiss the possibility that some who are called to eternal life through Christ Jesus are disqualified of eternal life and end up reprobate.

Even the apostle Paul said,

But I keep under my body, and bring it into subjection: lest that by any means, when I have preached to others, I myself should be ***a castaway.***

(1 Cor. 9:27 emphasis added)

Paul could easily have said *"lest I myself should be a reprobate,"* since the same Greek word *adokimos* is here translated as *castaway.* Why does Paul here speak of himself in this manner? Could Paul be speaking metaphorically of being *rejected, cast aside, or discarded as a potter's vessel,* after he had labored so long preaching to save others?

In the book of Romans, *Paul uses a metaphor of the potter and the clay to illustrate God's mercy, compassion, and longsuffering toward us.*

For the scripture saith unto Pharaoh, Even for this same purpose have I raised thee up, that I might shew my power in thee, and that my name might be declared throughout all the earth. Therefore hath he mercy on whom he will have mercy, and whom he will he hardeneth. Thou wilt say then unto me, Why doth he yet find fault? For who hath resisted his will? Nay but, O man, who art thou that repliest against God? Shall the thing formed say to him that formed it, Why hast thou made me thus?

Hath not the potter power over the clay, of the same lump to make one vessel unto honour, and another unto dishonour? What if God, willing to shew his wrath, and to make his power known, endured with much longsuffering the vessels of wrath fitted to destruction: And that he might make known the riches of his glory on the vessels of mercy, which he had afore prepared unto glory.

(Rom. 9: 17-23)

The Bible is full of examples of God's dealing with men who *knew God,* yet *they glorified him not as God* because of their *hardness and impenitent heart* (Rom. 1:21, 2:5). Some who come to mind are *Cain, Esau, Nimrod, Pharaoh, King Saul, and Judas Iscariot.*

In the case of Pharaoh, Paul says that God raised him up *to show his power and to declare his name throughout the earth.* Paul then attributes *the hardening of Pharaoh's heart* to God, and intimates that this was possible only after God had *endured with much longsuffering the vessels of wrath fitted to destruction.* He likened Pharaoh to *potter's clay in the hand of God.*

This provides an illustration of *what actually happens to a person's heart that continually resists the efforts of God to revive him and bring him to a place of repentance before it is too late.*

The Potter's House

Then I went down to the potter's house, and, behold, he wrought a work on the wheels. And the vessel that he made of clay was marred in the hand of the potter: so he made it again another vessel, as seemed good to the potter to make it. Then the word of the LORD came to me, saying, O house of Israel, cannot I do with you as this potter? saith the LORD. Behold, as the clay is in the potter's hand, so are ye in mine hand, O house of Israel.

(Jer. 18:3-6)

Woe unto him that striveth with his Maker! Let the potsherd strive with the potsherds of the earth. Shall the clay say to him that fashioneth it, What makest thou? or thy work, He hath no hands?

(Isa. 45:9)

God sent Jeremiah the prophet to *the potter's house.* There he waited for a word from *the LORD.* As he waited, he watched the potter mold a vessel from a fresh yet crude lump of clay. During this process, something interesting happened. The vessel the potter made became marred or blemished while in his hands.

Therefore, the potter began to mold it again into something else. Re-throwing the clay, shaping and reshaping, removing pebbles and such—his skillful hands applying the right amount of pressure, for the right amount of time in all the right places. Sometimes he adds something such as water or straw to give his creation a certain texture or character, until finally he has a vessel that will survive the trial of fire and be forever finished. The point I want to make here is:

The potter cannot continue his work indefinitely. The physical properties of the clay have limitations and determine how long this process of molding and shaping can occur and whether the potter will be successful.

We must understand that these limitations do not exist with the potter but with the clay. The potter must fashion the vessel while the clay is still pliable enough to respond to *the hand and the will* of the potter.

If the clay's character is such that it resists the will of the potter, it will after time harden and become brittle.

Once the clay hardens to a certain degree, the vessel is no longer able to respond to the potter's efforts to mold and fashion it as he designed. Like Pharaoh, the vessel has become *reprobate,* a vessel *of wrath fitted to destruction. Disapproved and rejected,* they are now as Paul said, *a castaway,* (Gk. *adokimos*) *and* will end up discarded in the potter's field.

Such is also the end of those who *fall away* from *the faith* and are *past the point from which they will not return.* You may ask:

Why can't they return or renew themselves to repentance (Heb. 6:6)*?*

Like the potter's clay, *the reprobate's heart has now been hardened through pride, presumption, stubbornness, and rebellion.* Because of these things, the reprobate has resisted all prior attempts of the *Holy Spirit* to remold him and lead him to conviction and repentance.

Though he may have believed and felt conviction at one time, he now has built *a wall of denial* around himself and *will not repent.* Because they have resisted the Holy Ghost, they have *no moral compass* to find their way back (Acts 7:51). Paul says this of those who depart from the faith: "Their conscience [is] seared with a hot iron" (1 Tim. 4:1-2). It is *cauterized* (Gk. *kausteμriazoμ*)*, branded, or rendered insensitive.* It no longer functions as God intended and ***the reprobate in effect has no conscience.*** *He can no longer discern right from wrong. His ability to choose right from wrong has been compromised. He no longer feels conviction of his sin and lifestyle.* He is *past feeling* (*Gk. apalgeao*) and has become *apathetic* (Eph. 4:19). Furthermore, because he has been given over to a reprobate mind, h*e has no spiritual understanding* (Rom. 1:29).

The Son of Perdition

While I was with them in the world, I kept them in thy name: those that thou gavest me I have kept, and none of them is lost, but

the son of perdition; that the scripture might be fulfilled.
(Jn. 17:12)

Wherefore that field was called, The field of blood, unto this day. Then was fulfilled that which was spoken by Jeremy the prophet, saying, And they took the thirty pieces of silver, the price of him that was valued, whom they of the children of Israel did value; And gave them for the potter's field, as the Lord appointed me.
(Matt. 27:8-10)

Take heed, brethren, lest there be in any of you an evil heart of unbelief, in departing from the living God. But exhort one another daily, while it is called To day; lest any of you be hardened through the deceitfulness of sin. For we are made partakers of Christ, if we hold the beginning of our confidence stedfast unto the end;

And to whom sware he that they should not enter into his rest, but to them that believed not? So we see that they could not enter in because of unbelief.
(Heb. 3: 12-14,18-19)

The way to the potter's field and becoming a castaway is long and full of well-marked detours back to Calvary, back to the blood, and back to the household of faith. Yet, how is it that a person's heart can become so darkened and so cold that he can step out into the night air and deliberately betray *the innocent blood* and sell his Lord for *thirty pieces of silver?* I am sure we have all asked, "Why did Judas do it?"

Although there is not much said in the gospels about Judas, what we do find is disturbing. It appears that Judas was given a place of trust among *the twelve* as the treasurer. John records, however, that Judas was " *...a thief, and had the bag, and bare what was put therein*" (Jn. 17:6). It seems that Judas was a covetous man and stole money from the bag.

The love of money and *an evil heart of unbelief* drove Judas to make a covenant of betrayal with the chief priests as he sought for an opportunity to betray Jesus (Matt. 26:15).

There is a difference between *saving knowledge* and *saving faith.* Judas, being one of the twelve, had an intimate saving knowledge of Christ. Yet, in spite of being a partner in Christ's ministry, seeing signs, wonders, hearing the word, performing miracles, etc., it appears:

Judas did not possess saving faith.

I believe that *Judas no longer believed in Jesus* and His claim to be the Messiah, and he became a *reprobate* only after his heart was hardened through *unbelief* and *the deceitfulness of sin* (Heb. 3:13).

The Bible warns that we should take heed "lest there be in any of you an evil heart of unbelief, in departing from the living God" (Heb. 3:12), and, "Let us therefore fear, lest, a promise being left us of entering into his rest, any of you should seem to come short of it" (Heb. 4:1).

The apostle John said *the unbelieving* shall have *their part* in *the lake of fire* (Rev. 21:8). No one should therefore be surprised that Judas ended up in *the potter's field—a castaway.* Yes, he did repent to the chief priests and took back the money, but *there is no record that he sought the forgiveness of God.* Instead, he chose the ultimate act of selfishness; he committed suicide. He died *the son of perdition*—a reprobate.

Saul, The Rejected King

Then came the word of the LORD unto Samuel, saying, It repenteth me that I have set up Saul to be king: for he is ***turned back from following me,*** *and hath not performed my commandments.*
(1 Sam. 15:10,11, emphasis added)

For rebellion is as the sin of witchcraft, and stubbornness is as iniquity and idolatry. Because thou hast rejected the word of the LORD, he hath also ***rejected*** *thee from being king.*
(1 Sam. 15:23)

And the LORD said unto Samuel, How long wilt thou mourn for Saul, seeing I have ***rejected*** *him from reigning over Israel? fill thine horn with oil, and go, I will send thee to Jesse the Bethlehemite: for*

I have provided me a king among his sons.
(1 Sam. 16:1)

He, that being often reproved hardeneth his neck, shall suddenly be destroyed, and that without remedy.
(Prov. 29:1)

I want to examine briefly two additional Old Testament examples of reprobation. These have nothing to do with rejecting the gospel of Jesus Christ. These have to do with resisting God's will and purpose for one's life to the point of being *disqualified* and *rejected.*

One of the saddest tragedies in scripture is the rejection of Saul as king over Israel. This action was precipitated by Saul's *willful disobedience of God's Word on more than one occasion.* Saul began as a humble, obedient servant of God. Over time we can see how *pride, presumption, stubbornness and rebellion* led Saul to behavior, which caused him to be ***rejected*** (Hebrew. *ma' ac. reject, reprobate*). Because of these things,

God removed his Holy Spirit from Saul and rejected him as king over Israel and Judah (1 Sam. 16:14).

It is my opinion that Saul did not repent and died a reprobate. There may be reservation on the part of some as to whether Saul was eternally lost due to Samuel's remarks in 1 Samuel 28:19, "*and tomorrow shalt thou and thy sons be with me." However*, Samuel could simply mean that Saul would be in *Hades* among the dead. I can, however, state that Saul *turned back from following* the Lord. There were at least:

<u>*Four reasons Saul became a reprobate*</u>

- *Saul usurped the office of the priesthood* (1Sam. 13: 9-10)
- *Saul spared the life of King Agag, an Amalekite* (1Sam. 15: 8-9)
- *Saul sought to slay David, who was God's anointed* (1Sam. 19:1)

- *Saul consulted with the witch at Endor* (1Sam. 28:7-18)

Saul displayed the sin of *pride, presumption,* and *self-will* when he went into the priest's office and offered sacrifice instead of waiting for Samuel as he was instructed. Later, we find the sin of *rebellion* against God's leadership and *stubbornness* as he spared the life of Agag, tried to kill David, and consorted with witchcraft when *the Spirit of the Lord departed from* him and he could no longer hear from God (1 Sam. 16:14).

We should also note that to avoid being tortured and killed by the Philistines, Saul tried unsuccessfully to kill himself on the battlefield and is finally killed by an *Amalekite*. The irony here is that,

The sin that you allow to live in your life today could be the thing that destroys you tomorrow.

Rebellion against God and spiritual leadership is a very serious thing and can result in apostasy and hardening of the heart.

Dabbling in, consorting with witchcraft, and embracing the occult after walking in truth can also lead one down the road to becoming a reprobate. When one becomes a reprobate—as with Saul—it is as if *the Spirit of the Lord* departs from him.

Esau, The Rejected Son

And Jacob said, Sell me this day thy birthright. And Esau said, Behold, I am at the point to die: and what profit shall this birthright do to me? And Jacob said, Swear to me this day; and he sware unto him: and he sold his birthright unto Jacob. Then Jacob gave Esau bread and pottage of lentiles; and he did eat and drink, and rose up, and went his way: thus Esau despised his birthright.

(Gen. 25: 31-34)

Looking diligently **lest any man fail of the grace of God;** *lest any* **root of bitterness** *springing up trouble you, and thereby many be defiled; Lest there be any fornicator, or profane person, as Esau,* *who for one morsel of meat sold his birthright. For ye know how that afterward, when he would have inherited the blessing, he was* ***rejected:*** *for he found no place of repentance, though he sought it carefully with tears.*

(Heb. 12:15-17, emphasis added)

Our final example of a reprobate is Esau the son of Isaac, brother of Jacob. As the eldest son,

Esau was born to inherit the birthright consisting of:

- *The patriarchal blessing of Abraham*
- *The double portion of his father's inheritance*
- *The high priestly function within the family*
- *The royal line through whom the Messiah would come*

One would think that *the birthright* was something Esau would cherish. However, the Bible says that Esau *despised his birthright* (something of inestimable value) and one day he *sold it* to Jacob for a bowl of soup.

Some early insight into Esau's character reveals:

- *Esau did not have a heart for God.*
- *Esau did not love the things that God loves.*
- *Esau did not hate the things that God hates.*
- *Esau lived a life of self-gratification and self-indulgence.*

The Bible calls Esau *a profane man* and *a fornicator.* He *was a man of the field,* worldly and catered to his flesh. *He counted the birthright as something unholy, common, and to be despised.* He said to himself, "...what profit shall this birthright do to me?" (Gen. 25:32). Because of this attitude, God *rejected* him, even after he tearfully sought to change Isaac's mind. The Bible says, *he found no place of repentance.* After he was *rejected* (Gk: *apodokimazo — "to reject" as the result of examination and disapproval*), *rebellion and bitterness* led Esau down the road to reprobation.

I have seen on more than one occasion where bitterness has

caused some to backslide and harden their hearts against God. The writer of Hebrews mentions being *defiled* by a *root of bitterness.* It is my belief that bitterness can contaminate a person's spirit and can cause one to *fail* (Greek. *hustereo*) or *fall short* of the grace of God.

With spite, and to get even with his father for giving the birthright to Jacob, Esau became a fornicator. *Against his father's will, he deliberately sought to contaminate Isaac's seed by marrying a descendant of Ishmael, a woman of Canaan* (Gen. 28:6-9). This is hardly the attitude of one who is repentant.

The Unpardonable Sin

Verily I say unto you, All sins shall be forgiven unto the sons of men, and blasphemies wherewith soever they shall blaspheme: But he that shall blaspheme against the Holy Ghost hath never forgiveness, but is in danger of eternal damnation:

(Mark 3:28-29)

And whosoever shall speak a word against the Son of man, it shall be forgiven him: but unto him that blasphemeth against the Holy Ghost it shall not be forgiven.

(Luke 12:10)

Since a case can be made that a person *once enlightened* may *fall away* from ***the faith*** and may become *reprobate,* all scriptures that speak of such must refer *to* ***one who no longer believes in the blood atonement of Jesus Christ.***

When one who has been made a partaker of the Holy Ghost, and through apostasy, unbelief, and hardness of heart, renounces or denies the person and work of the Holy Spirit in redemption, he or she runs the risk of committing a sin of blasphemy against the Holy Ghost—a sin for which there is no forgiveness.

Paul writes of those *who resist the truth,* that they are *men of corrupt minds,* and are *reprobate concerning the faith.* He also mentions those who "*...concerning faith have made shipwreck: Of whom is Hymenaeus and Alexander; whom I have delivered unto*

Satan, that they may learn not to blaspheme" (1 Tim. 1:19-20; 2 Tim. 3:8).

Some believe that the unpardonable sin cannot be committed today because Jesus is no longer physically upon the earth performing miracles. Therefore, no one can ascribe the works of Jesus to the power of Satan. Those who embrace this view usually teach that the age of miracles is past. However, I submit for your consideration that:

Though Jesus is not here in body, He is here in Spirit. Through the person of the Holy Spirit, Jesus is performing greater miracles through believers today.

There are many early church examples of Jesus healing and performing miracles through believers after his resurrection. When Peter said, "Aeneas, Jesus Christ maketh thee whole: arise, and make thy bed,"(Acts 9:34) he was speaking in the name of Jesus, and Aeneas was healed through *the power of the Holy Spirit* (Acts 9:33-34). This affirms that:

The Holy Spirit performs the works of Jesus through believers today.

If you believe the age of miracles did not cease with the *early church* and the apostles, then you must also believe *the unpardonable sin can be committed today.* Furthermore, I believe a sinner cannot commit the unpardonable sin.

The unpardonable sin can only be committed by one who has been in intimate fellowship with the Lord and his church.

This person must first ***depart*** from *the faith, deny or renounce the work of the cross,* "count the blood of the covenant wherewith he was sanctified, an unholy thing, and do despite unto the Spirit of grace" (Heb. 10:29).

In other words, in the end he or she has *insulted* or blasphemed the *Holy Spirit. One cannot deny the active participation of the Holy Spirit in accomplishing the redemptive work of Calvary and be saved.* Such denial or rejection is not only heresy, it is blasphemy. For it is written:

How much more shall the blood of Christ, who through the eternal Spirit offered himself without spot to God, purge your conscience from dead works to serve the living God?

(Heb. 9:14)

It is my belief that:

One who has committed the unpardonable sin will not be forgiven because his reprobate state of mind and an evil heart of unbelief leaves him incapable of repentance and faith toward God (Heb. 6:4-6)**.**

Can such be said to have *genuine saving faith* since he has:

- *departed from the faith?*
- *denied the blood atonement? and*
- *rejected the work of the Holy Spirit?*

I am of the persuasion that such incidents of one becoming a reprobate are extremely rare. Most of us have never met a true reprobate and probably would not even know it if we had. Perhaps we have encountered *prodigals, false prophets and teachers* (who were never in the truth to begin with), who have been labeled falsely as *reprobate.*

Finally, I want to add a word of *caution* against labeling anyone in the *Body of Christ* a *reprobate*. No one knows the heart of another.

It is my conviction that no one but God knows who is or who is not a reprobate.

The very use of the word "reprobate" should bring pause and carefulness since it implies that one is eternally lost with no hope of salvation.

If one is guilty of calling someone a *reprobate* whether in ignorance or intentionally, one should repent and take heed lest they label someone falsely. We are not to judge lest we be judged.

The Sin unto Death

If any man see his brother sin a sin which is not unto death, he shall ask, and he shall give him life for them that sin not unto death. There is a sin unto death: I do not say that he shall pray for it. All unrighteousness is sin: and there is a sin not unto death.
(1 Jn. 5:16-17)

Some believe that *the sin unto death* referred to in the first epistle of John is *the unpardonable sin.* However, I cannot support this view for the following reasons:

1) ***<u>The unpardonable sin</u>*** *is* a *specific sin of blasphemy against the Holy Spirit.* This sin will result in spiritual death because *one has reached a reprobate state of apostasy from which one will not recover.*

The mind, heart, conscience, and will is worthless or reprobate regarding spiritual things. This person has *denied the blood atonement, blasphemed and rejected the work of the Holy Spirit, dies in unbelief and hardness of heart,* and therefore will not be forgiven.

2) ***<u>The sin unto death</u>*** is *any sin that brings the discipline or chastisement of God, in which the bringing of such discipline results in the physical death of a believer.*

This person is **"a brother,"** believes in the Lord Jesus Christ and is saved. However, *this person is walking in disobedience to the revealed will of the Lord and has unconfessed or unrepented sin in their life.*

Ananias and Sapphira

Some may be asking the question, What about Ananias and Sapphira?

Ananias and his wife, Sapphira, are New Testament examples of believers who died a premature death because of the direct discipline of God due to unconfessed and unrepented sin in their lives.

Just what happened to bring about this tragedy?

But a certain man named Ananias, with Sapphira his wife, sold a possession, And kept back part of the price, his wife also being privy to it, and brought a certain part, and laid it at the apostles' feet. But Peter said, Ananias, why hath Satan filled thine heart to lie to the Holy Ghost, and to keep back part of the price of the land? Whiles it remained, was it not thine own? and after it was sold, was it not in thine own power? why hast thou conceived this thing in thine heart? thou hast not lied unto men, but unto God. And Ananias hearing these words fell down, and gave up the ghost: and great fear came on all them that heard these things. And the young men arose, wound him up, and carried him out, and buried him. And it was about the space of three hours after, when his wife, not knowing what was done, came in. And Peter answered unto her, Tell me whether ye sold the land for so much? And she said, Yea, for so much. Then Peter said unto her, How is it that ye have agreed together to tempt the Spirit of the Lord? behold, the feet of them which have buried thy husband are at the door, and shall carry thee out. Then fell she down straightway at his feet, and yielded up the ghost: and the young men came in, and found her dead, and, carrying her forth, buried her by her husband. And great fear came upon all the church, and upon as many as heard these things.

(Acts 5:1-11)

Each time I read the account of these first-century believers dying this way, I shudder and thank God for being so merciful to me through all of my shortcomings and failures. It took me a while before I could understand just what happened with Ananias and his wife. I believe the Holy Spirit has given me some insight. While it is true they were *"cut off,"*

The text does not say they were lost or that they went to hell.

This is assumed and is pure *speculation* on the part of many preachers. While it makes for good drama and is used by many legalists to intimidate believers to give faithfully to the church, etc., I am of the persuasion that these two were called home prematurely. That is, they died and went to heaven way before their time.

I know that sounds strange to some of you, as if God is rewarding them for their sin, but that is not so. Think about it. Apparently, they had already promised to sell their land and give the entire proceeds to the church (Acts 4:32-37). The reason they lied was to keep some of the proceeds so they could have more for themselves. They were, in effect, laying up treasure on the earth.

It is my belief that while their counterparts continued to live, serve God and lay up treasure in heaven, Ananias and Sapphira, due to their deception and covetousness, were denied the privilege of laying up treasure in heaven. They were called home early to face eternity with little or no treasure awaiting them.

In my opinion, Ananias and Sapphira committed a *sin unto death.* Although the discipline and judgment fell quickly and directly upon them, the church at large was meant to benefit from their example.

The apostle Paul, in his first epistle to the Corinthians, teaches that the chastisement of God can include the premature death of a believer.

Paul also warns of premature death along with sickness if we do not examine or judge ourselves and discern the Lord's body before partaking in the Lord's supper (1 Cor. 5:1-5, 11:28-32).

- *Paul alludes to the premature death of a believer who has un-confessed and unrepented sin in his life.*

- Paul teaches *premature death* is a *judgment* and the result of the *chastisement* of God.

- *Paul teaches that even Satan is employed as an agent of divine discipline to bring an erring believer to a*

> *place of repentance or premature death.* However, Satan cannot touch a believer's life without express permission of God (Job. 2:4-5).

If the believer in Jesus Christ will not repent, God may call an erring believer home prematurely:

- *to prevent the Body of Christ from being affected by sin*
- *to prevent unbelievers from blaspheming against God, and*
- *to prevent new converts from stumbling*

This does not mean, however, that the believer will go to hell. If so, Paul could not write the following:

For I verily, as absent in body, but present in spirit, have judged already, as though I were present, concerning him that hath so done this deed, In the name of our Lord Jesus Christ, when ye are gathered together, and my spirit, with the power of our Lord Jesus Christ, To deliver such an one unto Satan for the destruction of the flesh, ***that the spirit may be saved in the day of the Lord Jesus.***
(1 Cor. 5:3-5, emphasis added)

For he that eateth and drinketh unworthily, eateth and drinketh damnation to himself, not discerning the Lord's body. For this cause many are weak and sickly among you, and many ***sleep****. For if we would judge ourselves, we should not be judged.* ***But when we are judged, we are chastened of the Lord, that we should not be condemned with the world.***
(1 Cor. 11:29-32, emphasis added)

For example, the believer who committed fornication in First Corinthians, chapter five, *repented.* He was not called home prematurely, because he submitted to the discipline that he received from *the Lord* and the *Body of Christ* (See 2 Cor. 2:5-10).

After considering what the Bible says about backsliding, it is clear to me that God does not see the backslider the way many in the church do. Yes, the backsliding prodigal is indeed lost *but not in the sense of eternal damnation.* Like the parables of *the lost sheep, the lost coin, and the lost son*, he is simply *temporarily misplaced* or *temporarily out of God's perfect will* for his life (Lk. 15: 1-31). A prodigal who is not an apostate will be chastened of the Lord, called home prematurely, or he will return to the household of faith.

Even one who departs from the truth has a chance to repent and be converted. James says that such can be admonished, persuaded, and eventually *converted* or *turned from the error of his ways, if his heart is open* to godly leadership in his life. James writes of an apostate who has not yet become reprobate:

Brethren, if any of you do err from the truth, and one convert him; Let him know, that he which converteth the sinner from the error of his way shall save a soul from death, and shall hide a multitude of sins.

(Jas. 5:19-20)

In conclusion, the sin unto death is not a specific kind of sin. At least the apostle John does not give us any specific kind of sin to pray about above another. It is simply sin that is *seen* or known by other believers, who are now encouraged to *ask* or entreat the Lord and *intercede* in the behalf of a sinning believer. John teaches that:

The prayer of believers can "give life" or delay the chastisement of premature death from falling on the sinning believer who has not yet sinned unto (to the point of) ***death*** (1 Jn. 5:16-17).

Obviously, the sin that has already resulted in a believer's death is not to be prayed for since the believer has already been called home. The truth relayed here is that,

Believers are to pray for other believers who have exposed sin in their lives that God will grant them repentance before they are called out of this world in death.

Suicide

Some have suggested that *suicide* is the *sin unto death* reasoning that *one cannot ask for forgiveness after committing suicide. In order to believe this, one would have to assume that suicide is also the unpardonable sin,* since (in their opinion) there is no pardon for one committing suicide. However, we know that *the unpardonable sin is not suicide* because Jesus said,

Verily I say unto you, ***All sins shall be forgiven*** *unto the sons of men, and blasphemies wherewith soever they shall blaspheme: But he that shall blaspheme against the Holy Ghost hath never forgiveness, but is in danger of eternal damnation:*
(Mk. 3:28-29, emphasis added)

In light of this scripture, *there has to be a provision of pardon for suicide.* The fact that Judas and Saul committed suicide is merely coincidental and has nothing to do with their reprobate nature. It merely attests to the fact that *for some, suicide is the ultimate act of selfishness.* It is my belief that suicide is a horrific and tragic sin. Nevertheless,

Suicide is covered by the blood of Jesus and is pardonable if one believes in Jesus Christ, His finished work of atonement and is not a reprobate.

If a person committing suicide has *rejected* the blood atonement and the work of the Holy Spirit, this would indicate that he has a *reprobate or counterfeit faith* to begin with.

Oftentimes mental or terminal illness or extreme mental or emotional distress can cause one to commit suicide. The victim sees suicide as the only way to escape the pain of life, etc. In a way, suicide is also a premature death because it prevents God from working deliverance in the behalf of the believer. However, I believe God does not override any man's *free will* and the Holy Spirit is deeply grieved when a believer commits suicide.

If We Confess Our Sins

But if we walk in the light, as he is in the light, we have fellowship one with another, and the blood of Jesus Christ his Son

cleanseth us from all sin.

If we say that we have no sin, we deceive ourselves, and the truth is not in us. If we confess our sins, he is faithful and just to forgive us our sins, and to cleanse us from all unrighteousness. If we say that we have not sinned, we make him a liar, and his word is not in us.

(1 Jn. 1: 7-10)

Can all of the believer's sins be accounted and atoned for if they are not specifically mentioned in prayer?

Is it possible that a believer can remember each and every incidence of sin and transgression of God's Word, not to mention be disciplined enough to confess them daily that he or she may receive forgiveness?

Is it not a matter of fact that *our sins have already been paid and atoned for through the blood of Jesus?* If the believer's sins have already been atoned for, then why is the believer encouraged to confess them anyway? What do we mean when we say our sins are to be confessed? The Apostle John teaches us that,

Though we are believers, we all have a sin nature, and no one is above sin.

John also teaches:

There are two ways that believers are cleansed from sin and unrighteousness: walking in the light and confessing our sins.

***1) Walking in the light*:** As we *walk in the light* of the revealed truth of God's Word in a state of redemptive grace, the believer is *supernaturally* cleansed from sin, just as ultraviolet light naturally cleanses and destroys bacteria from living things.

***2) Confessing our sins*:** Confession is God's way of allowing us to *personally own and acknowledge our responsibility for our sinful nature and our personal sins.* Confession cleanses our heart of *all unrighteousness* and iniquity (sinful desires) while at the same time purging our heart and conscience of guilt (Heb. 9:14).

There are sins of *commission* and sins of *omission.* I believe that it is not necessary or even possible to confess each sin by name, as they are too numerable to remember. Nevertheless,

We must be instant in prayer to confess that we have sinned and that we are sinful by nature.

In this manner, *we confess our sins.* This does not mean, however, that we never name our sin specifically. Of course, *we should confess all sin the Holy Spirit reveals to us in prayer. A believer who walks in the light will regularly confess his sin and experience continual cleansing and intimate fellowship with the Lord.*

Repenting early and confessing our sin will:

- *Prevent sin from encroaching upon our fellowship with God*
- *Safeguard our prayer life and devotion*
- *Prevent the believer's heart from rejecting the truth*
- *Safeguard the believer's love for the truth*
- *Prevent the hardening of the believer's heart*
- *Safeguard the believer from the pitfalls of backsliding and apostasy*
- *Safeguard the believer from the sin of pride, presumption, rebellion, and bitterness*

To confess our sins is to personally acknowledge or to own responsibility for them before God.

One of the most beautiful prayers of repentance and confession is *Psalms 51.* I have prayed it many times. It is a prayer of King David, *a man after God's own heart* (Acts 13:22). King David prayed:

Have mercy upon me, O God, according to thy lovingkindness:

according unto the multitude of thy tender mercies blot out my transgressions. Wash me throughly from mine iniquity, and cleanse me from my sin. For I acknowledge my transgressions: and my sin is ever before me. Against thee, thee only, have I sinned, and done this evil in thy sight: that thou mightest be justified when thou speakest, and be clear when thou judgest. Behold, I was shapen in iniquity; and in sin did my mother conceive me. Behold, thou desirest truth in the inward parts: and in the hidden part thou shalt make me to know wisdom.

Purge me with hyssop, and I shall be clean: wash me, and I shall be whiter than snow. Make me to hear joy and gladness; that the bones which thou hast broken may rejoice. Hide thy face from my sins, and blot out all mine iniquities. Create in me a clean heart, O God; and renew a right spirit within me. Cast me not away from thy presence; and take not thy holy spirit from me. Restore unto me the joy of thy salvation; and uphold me with thy free spirit. Then will I teach transgressors thy ways; and sinners shall be converted unto thee.

(Psa. 51:1-13)

Some have wondered why God continued to bless David even after he committed *adultery and murder.* King Saul did not commit the sins of David, yet David did not become a reprobate. Why? I believe it is because:

David walked in the light of God's Word and confessed his sins early.

When confronted by Nathan the prophet *David owned his own sin and did not make excuse or justify his sin as Saul did.* David repented; therefore, David was not *rejected* and did not become a reprobate. Moreover, unlike Saul, when David needed direction of the Lord, he did not turn to the dark side and consort a witch. David walked in the light of God's Word. He sought out Abiathar the priest and asked for the *ephod* whereupon were the *Urim* and *Thummim* and he inquired of the Lord (1 Sam. 23:9-11).

In conclusion, *Jesus died and shed his blood once for all.* Because of *one offering* for sin, we benefit from the *merit* of that sacrifice for eternity.

The blood of Jesus continually cleanses our heart and purges our conscience of the guilt of sin as we keep a repentant heart and walk before Him.

In this manner, we enjoy unbroken fellowship with the Father, the Son, the Holy Spirit and with each other (1 Jn. 1:3).

Part V

APPROACHING THE THRONE OF GRACE

17

The Grace Factor

And lest I should be exalted above measure through the abundance of

the revelations, there was given to me a thorn in the flesh, the messenger of Satan to buffet me, lest I should be exalted above measure.

For this thing I besought the Lord thrice, that it might depart from me. And he said unto me, My grace is sufficient for thee: for my strength is made perfect in weakness.

Most gladly therefore will I rather glory in my infirmities, that the power of Christ may rest upon me.

Therefore I take pleasure in infirmities, in reproaches, in necessities, in persecutions, in distresses for Christ's sake: for when I am weak, then am I strong.

(2 Cor. 12:7-10)

It is one thing to write about something you have read about but not experienced. It is quite another to write about something you have experienced first hand. I come to you not as one *on the outside looking in,* but as one personally *restored* through the *sovereign grace* of God.

To me, God's *grace* is not an *ideal* we strive for, or something we vaguely preach. *Grace* is something we must all experience on a daily basis. Sooner or later, we may realize that *without God's grace we would soon perish in our own corruption, hopelessness, and despair.*

Fresh Grace

Give us this day our daily bread.
(Mt. 6:11)

Give us day by day our daily bread.
(Lk. 11:3)

For this thing I besought the Lord thrice, that it might depart from me. And he said unto me, My grace is sufficient for thee: for my strength is made perfect in weakness.
(2 Cor. 12:8-9)

Jesus said, "I am the living bread which came down from heaven" (Jn. 6:51). In many ways, *grace* is like *manna,* the *bread of heaven* that sustained the children of Israel forty *years* in the wilderness (Ex. 16:13-36).

God wanted Israel to know that they would have to depend upon His goodness, mercy, and provision on a ***day by day*** *basis.*

To ensure this, God gave them a daily reminder. He miraculously supplied them with *only enough manna* to sustain them for one day. Before a *Sabbath,* they gathered twice as much. *If they tried to store it, it bred worms and stank.* Each person gathered *according to his eating* or as much as he required. It was *fresh* and was supplied each day. *Grace* is like *manna*:

- *We receive grace* ***daily***
- *We receive grace* ***freely***
- *We receive grace* ***sufficiently***

When Jesus said, "***Give*** *us this day our* ***daily*** *bread,*" could he have been alluding to the *daily bread* the children of Israel *freely* received from God who met *all* of their needs in the wilderness? As the *manna* was *new* every morning, each day the believer is *freely* supplied *fresh grace* sufficient to sustain him through all of his needs.

When we pray, "*Give us this day our daily bread,*" it is a cry for *fresh grace,* without which we cannot be sustained. *The believer does not have to work for it or earn it.* It is *free*. It is not something we deserve. The believer is simply encouraged to *believe, ask, and receive.*

Mercy, forgiveness, divine enablement, and strength to walk in our gifts and calling flow from the throne of grace to the believer.

When Paul besought the Lord to remove a certain temptation from him, God's answer to Paul was,

... my grace is ***sufficient*** *for thee: for my strength is made perfect in weakness.*

(2 Cor. 12:9, emphasis added)

I believe He was saying to Paul:

"Paul, my grace is all you need, and I will give you more than enough. My grace is stronger than all of your weaknesses, shortcomings, failures, and disappointments. I have given you grace that will abound beyond all of your need."

It is my belief that God equips the believer through grace.

To have God's *grace* is to have ***" the power of Christ ... rest upon"*** the believer (2 Cor. 12:9, emphasis added). We can only experience this *power resting upon us* in fullness as we *acknowledge our weakness and our utter dependence* upon Him.

Grace and Ministry

But by the grace of God I am what I am: and his grace which was bestowed upon me was not in vain; but I laboured more abundantly than they all: yet not I, but the grace of God which was with me.

(1 Cor. 15:10)

For the gifts and calling of God are without repentance.
(Rom. 11:29)

I would like to address briefly the subject of *grace, works, and ministry.* Since this subject will be covered in another book to be released later, I will only touch on a few things here. There are some in the *Body of Christ* who believe in *performance-based* ministry. This is the belief that:

God bestows gifts, callings, blessings, favor, and ministry based on human merit and the believer's works or performance.

I would like you to consider *two* questions I have asked myself:

***1)** Does God choose a man or woman for service based on works and human merit or on the basis of His grace?*

***2)** Does God give gifts, callings, or supernatural endowment on the basis of human merit (works) or on the basis of His grace?*

Paul said, "But by the grace of God I am what I am:" (1 Cor. 15:10). To hear some people preach, you would think that God made a mistake when He called the following men:

- *Abraham*—a liar (Ex. 20:16)
- *Moses*—a murderer (Ex. 20:13)
- *David*—an adulterer (Ex. 20:14)

That's just to mention a few. Although God mightily used these men, they were not perfect from a moral or legal standpoint. They *bore false witness, killed, coveted another man's wife, and committed adultery*. However,

God did not qualify them as prophets or leaders based on their individual merit. Nor did He disqualify them because of their failures.

Nevertheless, God used them *in spite of* their shortcomings. In fact, from what I have seen and heard in recent years, I doubt that they would be *card-carrying preachers* in some circles today. It is therefore evident to me that:

All New Testament ministry is the result of God's grace.

Whether *five-fold* ministry gifts, *body-ministry* or *service* gifts, or the *nine* spiritual gifts, they are all *gifts* (Gk. *charisma*) and the result of the *labor* and working of the *grace* of God. As I examine the scriptures, I cannot therefore endorse *performance-based* theology and ministry.

One cannot earn by human merit a gift of ministry, any more than one can earn by human merit the gift of salvation.

God *does not* give gifts to the redeemed because we are *holy, spiritual, or based on merit. That is why they are called* **gifts**. We may indeed be *holy*, we may indeed be *spiritual*, and we may indeed have *done righteous works.* However, it is important that we understand:

Believers do not and cannot deserve gifts from God of any kind based on our righteousness, obedience, good works, or performance.

God bestows *gifts and calling* purely based on His *love, grace, and according to His good pleasure and eternal purposes.* These operate through *faith*, and He asks that we *use them responsibly* and that *we live responsibly*. Furthermore, according to the apostle Paul, and contrary to modern thought and practice, these *gifts and callings* are *irrevocable.*

For the gifts and calling of God are without repentance.
(Rom. 11:29)

That is, through *grace*:

Once God places a divine call on a believer's life, He does not

change His mind.

A reasonable question may be asked: How does a person's character and reputation affect his gifts and calling?

A person's character and reputation may or may not affect his effectiveness and fruitfulness, but the gifts and calling are not revoked.

I know this is a difficult truth for the *legalist* to understand and accept, since he believes in *performance-based* theology and ministry. It is possible that someone may have a great call upon their life, great gifting, and great anointing upon their ministry. Yet, privately they may be struggling with sin. The reason why God continues to bless and honor the *gifts and calling* upon their life is not because they can *preach, win souls, build churches, touch and reach thousands, produce results, or otherwise perform.* It is because:

The gifts and calling are not based on human merit but upon God's grace, love, and eternal purposes.

You can be assured, however, that the *Holy Spirit* will convict and deal with this individual to bring him to a place of repentance as with any other believer.

Legalism and Ministry

The legalist believes that God will only bless and anoint the ministry and gifts of those who maintain a certain *standard* of *personal righteousness.* Furthermore, he believes God will remove His *anointing* and *revoke* the *gifts and calling* of those who do not. This all seems reasonable to the legalist. However,

The legalist is forgetting that God did not grant the gifts and calling through human merit in the first place.

There are at least *seven* Greek words translated as ***gift*** or ***gifts*** in the New Testament. The *five-fold* ministry *gifts* of ***apostle, prophet, evangelist, pastor* and *teacher*** are *gifts* (Gk. *doma*), or ***presents*** to the church. This means that although the *five-fold* ministry gifts are individual *charisma* gifts to the *five-fold minister,* they are "*presents*" (Gk. *doma*) to the church at large.

The *gifts and calling, five-fold ministry gifts, body-ministry* or *service gifts,* and *the nine* spiritual *gifts* are all "*charisma*" (Gk. *gifts*). This means they are ***a gift of God's grace*** (Gk. *charis*) and have *nothing whatsoever* to do with *merit, works, or performance* (Rom. 11:29, 12: 6-8; 1 Cor. 12: 27-31; Eph. 4:11-12).

The Principle of Abounding Grace

Moreover the law entered, that the offence might abound. But where sin abounded, grace did much more abound: That as sin hath reigned unto death, even so might grace reign through righteousness unto eternal life by Jesus Christ our Lord.

(Rom. 5:20-21)

Everything we know about God reveals that he is absolutely holy and hates sin. It is written:

He that covereth his sins shall not prosper: but whoso confesseth and forsaketh them **shall have** *mercy.*

(Prov. 28:13, emphasis added)

This scripture promises us that *God will respond to repentance and faith, with mercy, forgiveness, and grace*. This book is a message of hope to those who have "come short of the glory of God" (Rom. 3:23).

Perhaps you have wondered why you (or someone you know) have struggled with *sin* and moral failure of some kind. However, after *repentance, and faith toward God,* you then experienced *great grace, mercy, and compassion* upon your life and ministry. Well then, you have discovered and experienced the *principle* of *abounding grace*. Paul writes:

... But where sin abounded, grace did much more abound:
(Rom. 5:20)

What shall we say then? Shall we continue in sin, that grace may abound? God forbid. How shall we, that are dead to sin, live any longer therein?
(Rom. 6:1-2)

The *principle of abounding grace* reveals that God's grace *abounds* to the degree that the *power* of sin will be *broken* in our lives, not so that we can keep on sinning. However, Paul is clearly saying that,

The power of God's grace is more powerful than the power of sin.

Allow me to illustrate *the principle of abounding grace* using the physical laws of *aerodynamics* and *motion*. These laws or *principles* govern the flight of an airplane. To put it simply:

The *law of gravity* holds a plane to the ground as the *law of inertia* causes the plane to remain at rest. In order for flight to occur, *these principles must be overcome.*

To accomplish this, a principle called *thrust* is provided by the plane's engines, propelling it forward at a speed *greater* than *the law of resistance* called *drag*. When the mass and speed of the aircraft reach a certain threshold, *the principle of lift* takes over allowing air pressure under the wing to be greater than the pressure above it.

As the *greater laws of thrust and lift overcome the lesser laws of gravity, inertia, and drag*, the phenomenon of flight occurs as the plane leaves the ground and soars into the air. It is now *free* to fly **because it has overcome the laws that bound it to the earth.**

Likewise, the *laws of sin and death* ***must*** give way to *the law of the Spirit of life* in Christ Jesus. Paul writes:

For the law of the Spirit of life in Christ Jesus hath made me ***free*** *from the law of sin and death.*
(Rom. 8:2, emphasis added)

Just as the *lesser laws* of *gravity, inertia, and drag* **cannot** overcome the *greater laws* of *thrust and lift,* even so:

*It is **impossible** for sin to overcome a true believer's life.*

Because of *the principle of abounding grace*, the believer is *made **free*** (Gk. *eleutheroo—exempt*) and is *made* to overcome sin through *the blood of the Lamb* (Jn. 8:32-36; Rev. 12:11). These spiritual principles cannot be refuted.

The legalist commonly argues that *grace theology* transforms into *license* and results in a *licentious* lifestyle of sin that profanes the things of God. Therefore, anytime someone stands up for *the gospel of grace,* the legalist bristles with caution and concern. Having formerly been a legalist for many years, I know their concern; however, I no longer share it because I understand and have experienced the *principle* and *power of abounding grace* in my own life. *"I've been there and done that."* The truth of the matter is:

Grace does not transform into license. Grace transforms into liberty and freedom.

What kind of freedom—freedom to sin and do as I please? Of course not. *God forbid!* It simply means—grace promises and delivers:

- *Freedom from the law of sin and death*
- *Freedom from the Law of Moses*
- *Freedom from the law of righteousness through works*

Just as an airplane experiences the challenges and struggles of the difficult *phase* from *taxi to lift-off,* believers (due to immaturity in Christ or other reasons) ***may pass through a phase*** in life where sin may increase. This is possible depending on the quality of the believer's fellowship with God.

Nevertheless, as the believer *grows in grace,* when the *power* and *principle of abounding grace* takes root and takes hold, it will *transform* the believer's life. Regardless of his present state of *disobedience, immaturity, or lack of fruitfulness,* the principle of *abounding grace is stronger than the principle of sin and will prevail in the believer's life.*

There will come a time when the believer yields his heart, mind, will and spirit to the Holy Spirit of God. Like the airplane, he will reach a threshold in his life when grace no longer allows sin to have dominion or rule in his life.

Another important point I want to make here is the following:

- ***Legalism*** breeds *self-righteousness, spiritual pride, boasting, guilt, despair, fear, intimidation, insecurity, and bondage.*

- ***Grace theology*** leads the believer to *righteousness, humility, faith, hope, love, peace, security, and liberty.*

As grace *believers, we honor God's Word because of the quality of our relationship* and not because of the *intimidation, insecurity, or fear of losing our* ***free gift*** *of salvation.* It is my belief that:

The law or principle of abounding grace must be firmly established in the heart of the believer if salvation and the security of the believer are to be fully realized as a finished work of Jesus Christ at Calvary.

Isaiah and the Throne

In the year that king Uzziah died I saw also the Lord sitting upon a throne, high and lifted up, and his train filled the temple. Above it stood the seraphims: each one had six wings; with twain he covered his face, and with twain he covered his feet, and with twain he did fly.

And one cried unto another, and said, Holy, holy, holy, is the LORD of hosts: the whole earth is full of his glory. And the posts of the door moved at the voice of him that cried, and the house was filled with smoke.

Then said I, Woe is me! for I am undone; because I am a man of unclean lips, and I dwell in the midst of a people of unclean lips: for mine eyes have seen the King, the LORD of hosts.

Then flew one of the seraphims unto me, having a live coal in his hand, which he had taken with the tongs from off the altar: And he laid it upon my mouth, and said, Lo, this hath touched thy lips; and thine iniquity is taken away, and thy sin purged. Also I heard the voice of the Lord, saying, Whom shall I send, and who will go for us? Then said I, Here am I; send me.

(Isa. 6:1-8)

For we have not an high priest which cannot be touched with the feeling of our infirmities; but was in all points tempted like as we are, yet without sin. Let us therefore come boldly unto the throne of grace, that we may obtain mercy, and find grace to help in time of need.

(Heb. 4:15-16)

Often, it is only after a time of *personal crisis* that God begins to reveal the *mysteries* of His *grace* to us. For Isaiah, it was the year King Uzziah died. For me it began in 1988. I was thirty years old and had been in the pastorate nine years. The church family was growing, a building program was nearing completion and my ministry was widely known in certain circles. Everything was fine except:

My wife, who had always been by my side since the day we married, had not returned from a three-month absence back east. She had traveled east to be with her mom who was gravely ill. A broken leg turned out to be more severe than anyone knew. It turned out to be bone cancer.

Although her dad was well and there were other grown siblings, she felt it was up to her to settle her mother's affairs. My mother-in-law went to be with the Lord three months later. She was a wonderful woman and I loved her.

After the funeral however, my wife did not return to me. She said she needed more time to put her mother's affairs in order. That sounded reasonable to me. So, I waited and waited. Three months turned into a year and a half. We had only been together three months during that time period, shortly before and shortly after the funeral services. It took me a while to realize that she had abandoned me and would not be coming back. Later, I received a couple of disturbing telephone calls from a mutual friend and a member of her family. I was devastated.

To complicate matters, on my way home from a church camp meeting, I was involved in a major car accident in which two other people and I were injured. This, however, did nothing to hasten her return to me.

With medical problems related to the accident and without my wife, I wanted to resign my pastorate, but the membership encouraged me to stay on. Therefore, I remained for another year.

Somewhere along the way my world began to show signs of stress. My pastor and father in the ministry counseled me *to "divorce her and go on; don't let it affect the church."* I was confused and did not know what to do.

When you are in such situations, you get plenty of advice but little if any help. Legalism was fine as long as I could keep all the rules (at least before man). I sported about a very fine suit of *fig leaves.* I had always prided myself as being *strong* and *straight as an arrow* in matters of holiness. I had a reputation among my peers as a pastor of a strong holiness church—a *"no-nonsense, get in, get out, or get run over" kind of preacher!*

Then the inevitable happened. I fell. I will not bore you with details, but it was in this setting that *my light and my salvation* would eventually spring forth. As I cried out to God in the darkness with tears, He said this to me:

"You are not strong. I am strong. You are weak."

Then He spoke to me about *the spirit of the law* and *the Spirit of grace*. Shortly thereafter, I began to shed my *fig leaves, one here and one there*. I began to preach *grace* from my pulpit and from the pulpit of anyone who would invite me. My church and preacher friends thought I had gone off the deep end. I remember telling the congregation one day, "*The old man* (the legalist) *doesn't live here anymore.*"

Carlas Dees, a very good evangelist friend came by and fed us a steady diet of *grace* preaching for several weeks. It seemed too good to be true. Some received it; others accustomed to the rigid *old man* did not. After a year and a half my wife returned in time to dedicate the building. I wish I could tell you everything turned out fine and we all lived happily ever after. However, quite to the contrary, we could not resolve our differences. I had reached out for help from organizational leadership, but none came. Shortly thereafter we separated; I resigned my church and began a *prodigal journey* that cost me everything I had labored so hard and so long for.

All this happened, but not before God sent a prophet to warn me. His name is *E. Moses Hightower,* a *grace preacher*. He was also my friend. I will never forget that day. He sat across from me and read to me a *word* the Lord had given him for me. Our wives were also present. It was a word reminiscent of God's word to *Nebuchadnezzar* (Dan. 5:17-31).

I do not recall everything, but I recall he prophesied to me about falling, and my name becoming a byword and a reproach among my brethren. He proceeded to tell me of the trials and pain that would come into my life unless I would forgive my wife. He also spoke of God's mercy and of a restoration when God had finished these things in me. I listened numbly and said to myself, *"The Word of the Lord be done."*

Within one month, I walked away from my marriage, my church, my ministry, my calling and my God. I had enough; I was never going to *speak anymore in his name* (Jer. 20:9). I was *angry, bitter, stubborn, and disobedient.* I spent quite a few years running from God, severely chastened in love as I went. I know what it is like living in *a prodigal's world.*

Through all of this, I never stopped trusting in the blood, Calvary and the power of God's grace.

I did, however, abandon the fanciful idea that I would be saved through my own merit. Moreover, I abandoned the belief system of those who do.

Wounded and afraid, where was I to go? I loved Jesus, I loved the church and I loved the gospel. I hated, however, the legalistic religious system to which I subscribed. It was inadequate and lacked what I desperately needed most—*mercy, compassion, and forgiveness.* Instead, there was only *judgment and condemnation.* There was no remedy and no restoration available.

Is there no balm in Gilead; is there no physician there?
(Jer. 8:22)

Therefore, naked and ashamed, I hid among the trees. However, I was not a tree; I was *a son* of God. God did not leave me there; He sought me out and delivered me out of the *mouth of the lion;* He clothed me with His righteousness and favor.

In January 1997, I walked into the *People of Harvest* Church in Indio, California. Gilbert Chavez, a man I perceived to be a prophet of God, is the pastor. Brother Gilbert walked down the aisle and began prophesying about my calling, my past, my wounds, etc. He then embraced me, with tears flowing down both our faces. I felt the arms of God around me as if I were the *prodigal* returned home. My life began again.

Shortly thereafter, God began to deal with me about this book and the *gifts and calling* upon my life. I remember those first few months of God's dealing with me about these things. I got very little sleep, as the Lord chose the *wee* hours of the morning to speak to me. As I lay before God weeping, the only thing I could feel was a sense of unworthiness and of being *undone.* Like Peter, I cried, *"Depart from me for I am a sinful man oh Lord* (Lk. 5:8)."

I questioned God, made excuse, and used my past failures to shrink back from the call He placed on my life. He would have none of my excuses. He told me that my message and ministry was:

- *The gospel of the grace of God* (Acts 20:28)
- *The restoration of the fallen* (Gal. 6:1)
- *The reconciliation of the Body of Christ* (Jn. 17:21)

He told me *not to be afraid* to speak openly about my failures, and through *compassion,* He would heal *many* believers of their *wounds* and the *hurt* of their *failures* and past. I reminded God *that I had fallen,* was *unqualified, unworthy,* and that *no one* would listen to me anyway. God then reminded me that:

- *He was sovereign in my life, not I.*
- *He was worthy in my life, not I.*
- *He would do the work in my life, not I.*

He told me that through my *testimony* He would be glorified. He revealed to me that there would be great sacrifice required of me. God has also shown me that I would be persecuted and the message of *salvation by grace apart from works* will be *rejected* and *spurned* by some. He also promised me that it would also be received by many. He has sent several prophets to me to confirm these things. One prophet even spoke of the *arrows* that would hit me, but they would not harm me. Be that as it may, *by the grace of God, I am what I am.*

Sovereign Grace

Many preachers do not understand *the principle of abounding grace.* Neither do they realize that *it is governed by God and not man.* They do not understand that when we speak of the *sovereign grace* of God, we are saying that:

God's grace is sovereign over all the affairs of our life.

How can this be? Unlike an earthly king, God is the *supreme ruler* of all there is in heaven and earth. His sovereignty cannot be challenged by man, devil, or angel. *God's sovereign grace* is grounded in the reality that He rules the affairs of the universe. More importantly:

God's sovereign grace is grounded in the very nature of God, which is love.

One cannot separate God's *sovereign grace* from His *universal sovereignty* or from His *love*. Therefore, as *mercy* is greater than *judgement* (Jas. 2:13), likewise, God has decreed that His *grace* is greater than any of His laws and demands. These include His demand for *holiness, justice, righteousness, etc.* Why? Because:

Through the atonement, God's sovereign grace alone has the power to satisfy God's demand of justice for sin, righteousness, and holiness. Moreover, through the atonement, God found a way to satisfy and express His love and mercy.

This is consistent with both God's *character* (God is holy) and God's *nature* (God is love). It is on this basis that the believer is encouraged to approach *the throne of grace*.

The Throne of Grace

Let us therefore come boldly unto the throne of grace, that we may obtain mercy, and find grace to help in time of need.
(Heb. 4:16)

Isaiah's vision is more than just a dramatic scene in heaven. When Isaiah saw the throne of God, he saw the *temple* in heaven. The throne in Isaiah's vision corresponds to the ***mercy seat*** or the lid of the *Ark of the Covenant.* It was located in *the most holy place, or holy of holies in the tabernacle in the wilderness* and in *Solomon's Temple.* We know this because holy angels *cover their faces* above the throne as above the ark. We are reminded the things on earth are *patterned* after things in heaven (Ex. 25:9; Heb. 8:5, 9:23).

Because of the harmony of God's *character* and *nature*, *the love of God* will always move to *cover* and *atone* for man's sin *in order to satisfy God's holiness* and bring man into *fellowship* with Himself. This is why *Calvary* had to happen—to provide man *a fountain for sin and uncleanness* (Zech. 13:1). Man, however, must *acknowledge* God as *sovereign, holy*, and man must *confess* that he is *undone* without God. Thus, we turn to Isaiah's vision.

<u>*God revealed at least four things to Isaiah*</u>

- The *sovereignty* of God
- The *holiness* of God
- The *grace* of God
- The *mercy* of God

There are those who contend that God will not use a man or woman who has sinned or otherwise failed, and that such are not fit for the ministry. This is interesting to me, because *somebody forgot to tell God that He could not use such people.* I read somewhere that:

For *all have sinned and come short of the glory of God.*
(Rom. 3:23)

It humbles and amazes me when I consider how we mortals have no concept of how *undone* we are in the presence of the Almighty God and the holy angels. Yet, we think nothing of comparing our works and righteousness with one another. The Bible says:

For we dare not make ourselves of the number, or compare ourselves with some that commend themselves: but they measuring themselves by themselves, and comparing themselves among themselves, are not wise.
(2 Cor. 10:12)

Let's face it—We all look good when we stand next to someone else whom we judge less worthy or righteous than we are. However, how would we look standing next to Jesus? That is what we all should be concerned with.

I cannot find much written about Isaiah's personal life or his failures, as we are not given any details of that sort. I do know this—when the prophet Isaiah was before the presence of the throne of God and the holy angels he experienced the awesome *holiness* of God and *confessed* he was a sinner *undone.* Because he was *undone, he literally expected judgment and condemnation, crying, "Woe is me."* He received neither. Instead, he *obtained mercy and found grace.*

Here am I; Send Me

What is interesting to me is that while Isaiah was *preoccupied* with his *shortcomings* and his being *undone,* God was not preoccupied with the prophet's shortcomings. God was intent on meeting a need in Isaiah's life and extending grace to the prophet.

I know what it is like to focus on one's inadequacies and not on what God desires to do in one's life. Sometimes, before God can send a believer to do His bidding, He has to deal with *issues* in the man or woman's life that require the application of *that which atones for the shortcomings in the believer's life*. Grace, mercy, and forgiveness are such things.

God had a purpose in visiting Isaiah. It is my belief that God had a greater work yet for Isaiah to do and the visitation of God had come to equip him for that work. It is only *after* the believer *confesses his sinfulness* and *weaknesses that* God can offer him cleansing and pardon. Notice Isaiah owned his own sinfulness and shortcomings. He did not blame anyone else for them. Likewise:

It is therefore necessary and important for the believer to own his sin and weaknesses and confess openly before God any area of his life and heart, so that he may obtain mercy and find grace to help him in the time of need.

An angel flew with a red-hot coal from *the altar of sacrifice and atonement* and *applied* it to the mouth of the prophet. Interestingly, notice how *God not only purged Isaiah's sin,* He also took away his *iniquity,* things that were in his heart. It was only after God revealed His *sovereignty, holiness, mercy, and grace*—and dealt with Isaiah's *issues*—that Isaiah was ready to hear from God.

Also I heard the voice of the Lord, saying, Whom shall I send, and who will go for us?...

(Isa. 6:8)

When Isaiah realized that God had purged him from his sin, he was then able to respond in *faith* to the commission God had for him. It was the purging and the taking away of Isaiah's sin, along with his willingness to be sent, that equipped him as a prophet.

Perhaps you are in a phase of life in which you find yourself struggling with the call of God.

Your weaknesses, feelings of inadequacy, and the legalistic expectations of man have caused you to shrink back.

Please allow Isaiah's vision to encourage you. *God is sovereign in your life.* He chooses whom He will–not because you have it all together, but because *He does.*

The more you rely on God's grace working in and through you, the less you will rely upon what you can do.

If God calls you, equips you and sends you, then you have *more than enough grace* to accomplish His will.

Esther and the Throne

When Mordecai perceived all that was done, Mordecai rent his clothes, and put on sackcloth with ashes, and went out into the midst of the city, and cried with a loud and a bitter cry; And came even before the king's gate: for none might enter into the king's gate clothed with sackcloth.

Again Esther spake unto Hatach, and gave him commandment unto Mordecai; All the king's servants, and the people of the king's provinces, do know, that whosoever, whether man or woman, shall come unto the king into the inner court, who is not called, there is one law of his to put him to death, except such to whom the king shall hold out the golden sceptre, that he may live:...

(Esther 4:1-2, 10-11)

Now it came to pass on the third day, that Esther put on her royal apparel, and stood in the inner court of the king's house, over against the king's house: and the king sat upon his royal throne in the royal house, over against the gate of the house. And it was so, when the king saw Esther the queen standing in the court, that she obtained favour in his sight: and the king held out to Esther the golden sceptre that was in his hand. So Esther drew near, and touched the top of the sceptre.

(Esther 5:1-2)

And Esther spake yet again before the king, and fell down at his feet, and besought him with tears to put away the mischief of Haman the Agagite, and his device that he had devised against the Jews. Then the king held out the golden sceptre toward Esther. So Esther arose, and stood before the king, And said, If it please the king, and if I have found favour in his sight, and the thing seem right before the king, and I be pleasing in his eyes, let it be written to reverse the letters devised by Haman the son of Hammedatha the Agagite, which he wrote to destroy the Jews which are in all the king's provinces:

(Esther 8:3-5)

Another example of *the power of grace* over *law* comes from the book of *Esther*. I believe the book of Esther is a wonderful *grace book* because it demonstrates the *sovereign grace* of God in the affairs of His people. In addition, *it typifies what happens when a believer approaches God in the spirit realm.* Two of the principal characters are *Mordecai* and *Esther.*

• ***Mordecai***: dressed in *sackcloth*, typifies *a legalist* attempting to approach the throne of God clothed in the *dead works of pride and self-righteousness*. However, ***it was not lawful*** for anyone to enter *the king's gate clothed with sackcloth.*

Because he *was not* properly attired, Mordecai never made it past the gate of the *outer court*. Therefore, his cries went unheard and his request could not be granted.

• ***Esther***: adorned in *royal apparel,* typifies *a believer justified by faith in the blood atonement* and clothed *in the righteousness of God.* Although under penalty of death, she *defied the law of the Medes and Persians.*

Queen Esther stood at the gate to the royal house and entered the *inner court.* Unlike Mordecai, Esther found *favor* (grace) in the eyes of the king, approached the throne, and was granted her request.

How does a young Jewish girl become the queen of Persia, *defy the law*, stand before a gentile king, and find *favor* to reverse the sentence of death upon her and her people? This is particularly of interest because it is written that *the law of the Medes and Persians* ***cannot*** be *altered* or *changed* (Dan. 6:12,15). However, in this instance it was changed.

One woman dressed in *royal apparel* obtained *favor* (*grace*) in the eyes of her king. Such favor that the *curse of the law* was removed from her people. In the first place, we must recall:

It was not lawful for Esther to enter the inner court uninvited.

Through *faith* she *defied* the law and would surely have been executed, but she *obtained mercy and found grace* to help in her time of need.

Do not discount the grace factor in God's dealings in your life.

Men and women who approach God in faith—clothed with the righteousness of Jesus Christ—get a different result than those who do not.

The law and legalism is great at revealing your faults and meting out condemnation and judgement. Just remember that it is short on mercy. When you fail, it cannot deliver you.

Yet, how often we find Jesus extending the *golden scepter* of *grace, compassion, forgiveness, mercy, healing, etc.,* only to find some *Pharisee* protesting ***"it is not lawful"*** to do this or to do that.

Because *Jesus dealt with man on the basis of grace*, He healed on the *Sabbath* and touched those who were ceremonially unclean. Thank God, Jesus is greater than the *Sabbath*, greater than *Moses,* and greater than the temple. He can grant pardon, cleansing, and do what the law cannot do.

Legalism does not have the power to do such things, but grace does.

Like Esther, we can boldly approach the throne of grace.

For what the law could not do, in that it was weak through the flesh, God sending his own Son in the likeness of sinful flesh, and for sin, condemned sin in the flesh:

(Rom. 8:3)

I'm Looking for a City

And it came to pass, as they journeyed from the east, that they found a plain in the land of Shinar; and they dwelt there. And they said one to another, Go to, let us make brick, and burn them throughly. And they had brick for stone, and slime had they for morter. And they said, Go to, let us build us a city and a tower, whose top may reach unto heaven; and let us make us a name, lest we be scattered abroad upon the face of the whole earth.

(Gen. 11:2-4)

By faith Abraham, when he was called to go out into a place which he should after receive for an inheritance, obeyed; and he went out, not knowing whither he went. By faith he sojourned in the land of promise, as in a strange country, dwelling in tabernacles with Isaac and Jacob, the heirs with him of the same promise: For he looked for a city which hath foundations, whose builder and maker is God.

(Heb. 11:8-10)

Shortly after the flood, in the land of Shinar *the descendants of Cain gathered in defiance and disobedience to the God of heaven.* With *bricks* and *slime* they set out to build *a city and a tower, whose top may reach unto heaven.* It later became known as *the Tower of Babel.* With Nimrod, a descendant of Cain, as their ruler, *Babel* (Babylon) was intended to become the *political, commercial, and religious* center of the world.

Originally, *Babel* meant *"the gate of God."* Nimrod intended *Babel* to become *the gate of God* or the *entrance* to heaven. To put an end to this rebellion against God's command to repopulate the whole earth, ***God came down,*** confounded their language and scattered them so that they would fulfill His will. Since then, *Babel* has come to mean *confusion*. This illustrates the truth that:

- *Legalism* ***is man trying to climb up*** *to save himself.*

- *Grace is* ***God coming down*** *to save man from himself.*

Jesus said:

Verily, verily, I say unto you, He that entereth not by the door into the sheepfold, but climbeth up some other way, the same is a thief and a robber.

I am the door: by me if any man enter in, he shall be saved, and shall go in and out, and find pasture.

(Jn. 10:1, 9)

The Bible is written in the *spirit* of *redemption.* It is about the redemption of man from the curse of sin and death. It is about the drama and process of that redemption. The *grace of God* is fully expressed in *His love and kindness toward us through Christ Jesus.*

Legalism *exposed* is religious humanism. This can mean nothing less than *man is his own savior.* It is man *striving* to be saved and to reach heaven through the merit of his own effort.

In addressing legalism in the *Galatian* church, Paul wrote:

Are ye so foolish? having begun in the Spirit, are ye now made perfect by the flesh?

(Gal.3:3)

Well said, Paul! It is *foolish* to practice the *craft* of *righteousness through works.*

- Let there be no misunderstanding—legalism is a dangerous virus within the *Body of Christ*. It is a curse.

- Let there be no misunderstanding—legalism crafts salvation as *a mixture* of *faith and works* or ***God + man = salvation.***

Anyone who looks outside of the grace of God and the blood of Jesus Christ and anyone who places any merit or worth in their own works of righteousness in order to be saved is a legalist.

Like the inhabitants of *Babel,* many believers today are confused due to the encroachment of legalism within the *Body of Christ*. It is interesting that in *the last days* Satan will again try to establish *a stronghold* of religious humanism within the church.

More and more preachers are saying *less and less* about *the blood* and *the finished work* of Christ, and are saying more about the necessity of believers *establishing their own righteousness in order to be saved.* Make no mistake about it:

Achieving righteousness and salvation through human merit is religious humanism. It is climbing up some other way (Jn. 10:1).

Unlike Noah and the descendants of Seth—Nimrod, like his forefather *Cain,* forsook *"the right way"* and embraced *religious humanism* as a way to get to heaven (2 Pet. 2:15). *Nowhere* is it said of Nimrod or the inhabitants of *Babel* that they ever worshipped God through *faith in the blood atonement.* Nimrod tried to establish *his own righteousness* and by doing so, he *did not submit himself to the righteousness of God.*

For they being ignorant of God's righteousness, and going about to establish their own righteousness, have not submitted themselves unto the righteousness of God. For Christ is the end of the law for righteousness to every one that believeth.
(Rom. 10:3-4)

In building the tower, the citizens of *Babel* attempted to reach heaven through their own works. However:

Brick for stone and slime for mortar demonstrate the inadequate and inferior substitution of works in the place of genuine enduring faith in the blood atonement.

Nimrod lived in a temporary city built by man (works) and destroyed by God. On the other hand, Abraham looked (faith) for an eternal city made and blessed by God. *Man will build nothing in heaven.* He will not be able to boast in anything of himself. All of his boasting will be in that which God Himself has wrought through Jesus Christ.

"It is Finished!"

For I have received of the Lord that which also I delivered unto you, That the Lord Jesus the same night in which he was betrayed took bread: And when he had given thanks, he brake it, and said, Take, eat: this is my body, which is broken for you: this do in remembrance of me. After the same manner also he took the cup, when he had supped, saying, This cup is the new testament in my blood: this do ye, as oft as ye drink it, in remembrance of me. For as often as ye eat this bread, and drink this cup, ye do shew the Lord's death till he come. Wherefore whosoever shall eat this bread, and drink this cup of the Lord, unworthily, shall be guilty of the body and blood of the Lord. But let a man examine himself, and so let him eat of that bread, and drink of that cup. For he that eateth and drinketh unworthily, eateth and drinketh damnation to himself, not discerning the Lord's body.

(1 Cor. 11: 23-29)

When Jesus therefore had received the vinegar, he said, It is finished: and he bowed his head, and gave up the ghost.

(Jn. 19:30)

I conclude this work with the most powerful and meaningful illustration of *salvation through grace alone* found anywhere in the *New Testament.* It is embodied in the two elements of "*the Lord's Supper,*" commonly called the *communion service.*

Christ himself instituted the Lord's Supper to be a memorial service commemorating His redemptive work on the cross.

In Paul's day, *the Lord's Supper* did not consist of a small cracker and a tiny glass of grape juice during a church service. At the church in *Corinth,* apparently *the Lord's Supper* was celebrated with a complete meal of food and wine. However,

The true meaning of the Lord's Supper was in jeopardy of being lost.

At *Corinth,* the communion service became disorderly. Some were hungry and sober while others were stuffed and drunken. The apostle Paul sought to correct this problem. If these symbolic elements lost their full meaning in Paul's day, without proper teaching could it also happen today?

It is the attitude of the believer's heart and mind while partaking in the Lord's Supper that the apostle Paul is primarily concerned.

Paul warns believers *against the profane practice of partaking without discerning the Lord's body.* This could mean that *believers are to be discerning of the needs of others in the Body of Christ. It could also mean that,*

Believers should be careful to reverence and distinguish the symbols of the body and blood of Jesus from a common meal.

These elements were to be sanctified in their hearts and minds as ***holy*** *because* ***they represent the finished work of Christ at Calvary***. This is important for all believers because,

The principles of **substitution and atonement** *are clearly revealed in the elements of the bread and the cup.*

- ***The bread*** represents *the sacrifice of Christ's body in* ***substitution.***

- ***The cup*** represents *the shedding of Christ's blood in* ***atonement.***

These two elements declare that from start to finish, Jesus

Christ alone is the architect of our eternal salvation.

Yet, how often *the Lord's Supper* is improperly used as a *legalistic barometer* to measure one's *self-righteousness,* while at the same time we *lose sight* of the *true meaning* of the *bread* and the *cup*. That is:

To remember what Christ accomplished in our behalf.

Yet, *there is nothing in the elements of the bread and the cup to suggest or remind us of* **what we have done or what we must do**, except—through *faith* with *thanksgiving* we are to discern *the Lord's body.* That is, when partaking in the Lord's Supper,

We must recognize the person of Christ and assign to His body and His blood the total value of their worth.

- Each time the believer partakes of the *bread* and the *cup* it is a *visible* and consistent reminder that *Jesus paid the price for the believer's salvation* ***in full,*** *with His own blood* (Heb. 9:12).

- Each time the believer partakes of *the bread* and *the cup* he is declaring that Jesus is ***the author and the finisher*** of his faith (Heb. 12:2).

- Each time the believer partakes of *the bread* and *the cup* it is to *"shew"* or *openly acknowledge and confess* the *merit* of Christ's death and ***His finished work*** at Calvary (1 Cor. 11:26).

- Each time the believer partakes of *the bread* and *the cup* it is to remind the believer that he is enjoined to a ***New Testament*** (covenant) based on ***grace*** and not on the works of *the law* (Matt. 26:28).

When understood in the light of God's grace, the symbolic meaning of the bread and the cup deal a fatal blow to legalism

***and the concept of salvation and righteousness through human merit* (works).**

Jesus said, "This do in remembrance of me" (I Cor. 11:24). To partake in this manner is to *acknowledge* that,

We are therefore **saved and secure** *because He paid the price of our salvation* ***in full*** *and obtained eternal redemption for us* (Heb. 9:12). *There is nothing else the believer can do through human merit* (works) *to augment and supplement His finished work.*

We are to do this *till he comes* (1 Cor. 11:26). It is on this basis that believers are admonished:

But let a man examine himself, and so let him eat of that bread, and drink of that cup. For he that eateth and drinketh unworthily, eateth and drinketh damnation to himself, not discerning the Lord's body.

(1 Cor. 11:28)

Again, this scripture is misinterpreted to suggest that only those who are *worthy* can partake of *the Lord's table* and those who are not *worthy* should not partake, lest they bring *damnation* upon themselves. The real issue here is:

On what basis does one become worthy?

We may approach the table of the Lord from Sinai or from Calvary.

•*When we approach the table from the vantage point of Sinai and the basis of our own righteousness, none of us are worthy.*

•*When we approach the table from the vantage point of Calvary and the basis of the righteousness of Christ, we understand that it is by* **grace** *that we are partakers of the virtue and merit of his body and of his blood.*

With this attitude and in this manner we ***are*** worthy. *Search your heart if you will—confess your sin and repent if you will.* However:

Do not look to your own righteousness or merit when you partake.

We are not partakers because we are righteous in ourselves. We are partakers because *He died* to make us *the righteousness of God in Him* (2 Cor. 5:21).

Finally, there will always be those who will cling to their *fig leaves*, *the fruit of the ground, brick and slime*, etc. These are but the *self-righteous works of their own hands* (human merit). Yet, they seem to forget or ignore:

From the Garden of Eden to the altar of Abel; from Mt. Moriah to the door posts of Egypt; from the Tabernacle in the wilderness to Mt. Calvary; from the millennial kingdom to the eternal age, the principles of substitution and atonement are clearly present.

They will forever remain constant and consistent reminders that it is only through *faith* in *the finished work* and the merit of the *blood of Jesus Christ, the Lamb of God,* that we will inherit the promise.

Throughout the Bible, there is one promise that is consistent and true:

"...when I see the blood, I will pass over you..."
(Ex. 12:13)

Lord Jesus,

I confess openly that I am a sinner. Thank You for dying on the cross in my place. I acknowledge that it is only through enduring faith in Your shed blood that my sins are forgiven, my name is in the Lamb's book of life, and my salvation is secure.

I acknowledge that I have done nothing, nor can I do anything to merit my salvation or maintain it by any works of righteousness of my own. It is a free gift of Your redemptive grace.

Lord, I pray for myself, for the Body of Christ, and for all who will come to trust You as Savior; that the veil of legalism and righteousness through human merit may be removed from our eyes. I also pray that we may see that the righteousness of God can only be achieved by trusting in Your blood and Your finished work of Calvary.

In Jesus' name,

Amen.

No weapon that is formed against thee shall prosper; and every tongue that shall rise against thee in judgment thou shalt condemn.

This is the heritage of the servants of the LORD,

***and their righteousness is of me**, saith the LORD.*

(Isa. 54:17, emphasis added)

References

Enhanced Strong's Lexicon, 1995. Logos Research Systems, Inc.

New Strongs Dictionary of Hebrew and Greek Words, 1996. Thomas Nelson, Inc.

Vine's Complete Expository Dictionary of Old and New Testament Words, 1984, 1996. Thomas Nelson, Inc.

For inquiries, you may contact the author:

Charles Smoot
P.O. Box 1463
Kihei, Hi 96753

CESMOOT@aol.com

Printed in the United States
25482LVS00002B/193-195

9 781591 609896